Fresh Baked

Fresh Baked

Over 80 tantalizing recipes for cakes,
pastries, biscuits and breads

Louise Pickford

hamlyn

note

note Both metric and imperial measurements have been given in all recipes. Use one set of measurements only and not a mixture of both.

Standard level spoon measurements are used in all recipes.

1 tablespoon = one 15 ml spoon

1 teaspoon = one 5 ml spoon

The Department of Health advises that eggs should not be consumed raw. This book contains dishes made with raw or lightly cooked eggs. It is prudent for vulnerable people such as pregnant and nursing mothers, invalids, the elderly, babies and young children to avoid uncooked or lightly cooked dishes made with eggs. Once prepared, these dishes should be kept refrigerated and used promptly.

This book includes dishes made with nuts and nut derivatives. It is advisable for those with known allergic reactions to nuts and nut derivatives and those who may be potentially vulnerable to these allergies, such as pregnant and nursing mothers, invalids, the elderly, babies and children to avoid dishes made with nuts and nut oils. It is also prudent to check the labels of pre-prepared ingredients for the possible inclusion of nut derivatives.

Ovens should be preheated to the specified temperature – if using a fan-assisted oven, follow the manufacturer's instructions for adjusting the time and the temperature.

First published in Great Britain in 2006 by Hamlyn,
a division of Octopus Publishing Group Ltd,
2–4 Heron Quays, London E14 4JP

ISBN-13: 978-0-600-61356-5
ISBN-10: 0-600-61356-9

A CIP catalogue record for this book
is available from the British Library

Printed and bound in China

10 9 8 7 6 5 4 3 2 1

Contents

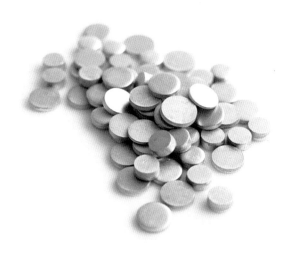

Introduction

This book contains a mouth-watering collection of cakes, breads, pastries, biscuits and slices, including such long-time favourites as French Apple Flan, Cottage Loaf and Classic Shortbread. Classics are given a modern twist – there are Kaffir Lime Tart, Mango and Palm Sugar Tatin and Rosewater and Cardamom Choux Buns. As well as these, you'll find some unusual recipes, such as Bacon and Beer Soda Bread and Coconut Cakes with Passionfruit Icing. There are also plenty of savoury dishes to choose from, including the traditional Beef, Oyster and Ale Pie, and aromatic breads, such as Pumpkin and Sage Bread, as well as pizzas and savoury muffins.

There is something incredibly comforting about the process of home baking. The process seemingly belongs to a different age, but even today it holds many of us in awe: the magic of yeast as it transforms a simple dough to a light and airy loaf or the layers of buttery puff pastry holding captive a filling of velvety custard and fresh summer fruits. It hardly seems possible that a few simple ingredients can create such a myriad of amazing cakes, breads, pastries and biscuits.

With so much choice in shops today it's surprising that we still bake at home. But, despite our hectic lifestyles and busy schedules, many of us still find time because baking is fun, rewarding and, most importantly, it gives us control over the quality of food we eat. Many commercial products tend to taste mass-produced and to be too sweet and ersatz. Home-baked cakes are rich with butter, and pastries melt in the mouth. Bread still warm from the oven emits mouth-watering aromas as it is torn open and slathered with butter, and cookie jars brimming with a variety of homemade biscuits make morning coffee a real occasion.

Baking doesn't have to be laborious or time consuming. Food processors and electric mixers take the hard work out of the process, and although some cooks may pour scorn on it, this equipment will reduce preparation times and the results are just as good. Of course, the traditional methods of mixing by hand will never go out of fashion, but at least we have a choice.

Baking has a long and fascinating history, and has become part of everyday life in many cultures around the globe. This book celebrates the art of home baking and is packed full of delicious recipes offering a wide array of baked goods for any occasion as well as all the useful information you need to get you started. So whether you are a beginner or an experienced baker, there is something here for everyone.

Ingredients

All types of baking share the same few basic ingredients: flour, fat and a liquid, usually water, to bind, with the addition of eggs and sugar. Without these ingredients we wouldn't be able to bake, so it makes sense to understand them and the role they play.

flour Bread flour (also called strong flour) is used mainly in yeasted breads. It is milled from the hardest types of wheat because of the high gluten content. During the kneading process gluten produces an elastic web of strands that trap the bubbles of carbon dioxide gases given off by the fermentation of the yeast. It is strong enough to prevent the gases from breaking

through the dough and escaping, allowing it to rise both before and during baking. It is available as white, wholemeal and granary. Other types of flour, made from different grains, such as rye, buckwheat and oatmeal, can be used in bread making but only in combination with wheat flour because they don't contain enough gluten to be used on their own.

Plain flour, which is used in quick breads, cakes, pastries and biscuits, is also milled from hard wheat. It contains a high proportion of gluten but not enough to be used in yeasted breads. Plain flour is combined with baking powder to leaven quick breads, cake batters and biscuit dough. It is available as both white and wholemeal.

Self-raising flour is plain flour that has already had a baking agent and salt added. It is only suitable for use in quick breads, cake batters and some biscuit doughs. It should never be used in yeasted breads. It is available as both white and wholemeal.

fat Used to bind, shorten and flavour baked items, fat can be either a solid fat, such as butter, margarine or vegetable fat, or a liquid such as oil. Butter is the best fat to use for most types of baking because of its superior flavour. Use unsalted butter for sweet items and salted butter for savoury recipes. Olive oil and sunflower oil are sometimes used in bread dough, cake batters and biscuits.

sugar Sugar sweetens, flavours and adds moisture to baked items. Although both granular and liquid sugars are used, it is important to use the sugar specified in a recipe because the results will vary significantly.

yeast Yeast is used to leaven dough, and it is responsible for giving bread its characteristic chewy texture and flavour. Three types of yeast are available: fresh, active dried and fast acting. The first two must be dissolved in a liquid before they can be mixed with flour, but fast-acting yeast can be added directly to flour (or blended with water).

All the recipes in this book are made using fast-acting yeast because it is the most widely available. If you want to use another type of yeast, remember that 1 x 7 g (¼ oz) sachet fast-acting yeast = 15 g (½ oz) fresh yeast = 1 tablespoon dried active yeast.

When you are using fresh or dried active yeast you must dissolve them first in warm water with a little flour to help activate them. Once combined, this 'sponge' is left in a warm place for 10 minutes until it is frothy. It is then ready to be added to the remaining flour for kneading. All types of yeast are killed at high temperatures.

eggs Eggs are used to bind, to add moisture and colour and to leaven baked items. Store eggs in the refrigerator but always remove them from the refrigerator at least 45 minutes before using to allow them to return to room temperature.

liquid Liquid is needed to lubricate bread dough, cake batters, pastry and biscuit dough, and it can take the form of water, milk, eggs, butter, oil, liquid sugars and citrus juice. Always use the type and amount of liquid specified in a recipe.

Baking techniques

bread Yeast breads, which are leavened, as the name suggests, with yeast, can be simple or elaborate, and they may be flavoured with herbs and spices, vegetables or cheese. Sweet breads are enriched with butter and eggs and may also be flavoured with spices, nuts and fruits.

Quick breads require less time because they are made using a chemical raising agent and are baked at once. They have a more porous texture than yeasted breads but can also be flavoured with nuts, spices, herbs and cheese.

Both types of bread are shaped and cooked either on a baking sheet or pressed into tins.

successful bread making

- Liquids should always be warmed until they are tepid to help activate yeast.
- If dough feels dry when it is first mixed add more water a tablespoon at a time; if it feels very wet add more flour a tablespoon at a time.
- To knead by hand, use the heel of your hand to push the dough out from the centre away from you, turning the dough a little each time.
- Dough should be left to rise in a draught-free place in a large, oiled bowl until it has doubled in size.

- Lightly dust the work surface when kneading or rolling dough.
- When you are scoring dough use a sharp knife and cut down without tearing.
- To test if yeast bread is cooked tap gently underneath. It should sound hollow. If not, continue cooking for 5 minutes and retest.
- Test quick breads by inserting a skewer in the centre and remove. It should come out clean. If not, continue cooking for 5 minutes and retest.
- When it is cooked always transfer bread to a wire rack to cool.

storing bread Store cooked bread for up to 24 hours in a paper or cloth bag in a cool place, but not the refrigerator. To freeze bread wrap it in clingfilm and then put this in a freezer bag. Defrost to room temperature and slice as normal.

cakes A cake is a sweet batter made from a combination of flour, fat, sugar and eggs, which is placed in a tin and baked. Cakes can be flavoured with a huge array of ingredients, from chocolate and coffee, to fruits, nuts, citrus, alcohol and many more. The three main cake methods are creaming, whisking and melting-in.

Creamed cakes are made by beating the butter and sugar together first before the eggs are added. The remaining ingredients are folded in, and the cake is baked. This produces a rich, buttery cake with an even, crumbly texture.

Whisked cakes are made when the eggs and sugar are whisked together over steaming water until the batter thickens and the ribbon stage is reached (see below). The remaining ingredients are gently folded in, and the cake is baked. This produces a particularly light cake with a firm, golden crust. Sometimes the yolks and sugar are beaten together first, and then the whites are whisked separately, giving the cake more stability.

Melted-in cakes are made when the butter and sugar are melted together before being stirred into the remaining ingredients and then baked. These cakes are usually dense and moist and keep well.

successful cake making

- When you add eggs to a creamed mixture add gradually, beating well after each addition. If the creamed mixture starts to curdle, sift in a little of the flour alternately with each addition.
- The ribbon stage for whisked cakes is reached as soon as the beaters, when lifted from the batter, leave a thick ribbon-like trail behind.
- When whisking egg whites make sure that both the bowl and the beaters are clean and dry, otherwise they will not aerate properly.
- Always sift the flour and raising agent together so they are evenly dispersed.

- Fold dry ingredients into a cake batter with a large metal spoon. Work gently from the centre of the bowl outwards, turning the bowl a little with each fold.
- If a cake batter is thick it will require spreading flat with a palette knife before baking. For cakes that take more than 1 hour to cook, always make a shallow indentation in the centre of the batter to allow for even rising.
- Never open the oven door during the first half of the cooking time. Thereafter, open and close the door gently.
- To test if a cake is cooked insert a metal skewer in the centre, wait 3 seconds and remove. It should be clean and dry. If not, return the cake to the oven and test again after 5 minutes.
- Leave cakes to cool in their tins for at least 5 minutes then transfer them to a wire rack to cool.

storing cakes To store a cake wrap it loosely in foil and keep it in an airtight container in a cool place for two or three days. Rich fruit cakes will keep longer. Sponge cakes can be frozen, wrapped in clingfilm, before they are filled or iced and defrosted at room temperature before icing.

pastry Pastries come in many guises, ranging from tart cases with their sublime fillings, pies with their golden crusts encasing soft fruits or savoury stews, to little feathery morsels rolled or layered with nuts, dried fruits and fragrant spices.

shortcrust pastry Shortcrust pastry, which is made with half the proportion of fat to flour, produces a crisp, light pastry, which is particularly versatile because it can be used in both sweet and savoury dishes. Increasing the ratio of fat to flour and adding either an egg yolk or a whole egg to shortcrust dough makes it rich shortcrust. This

produces a slightly more robust pastry case, ideal for those pastries not eaten straight away. The addition of sugar produces a softer dough, known as sweet shortcrust, which requires chilling for a minimum of 30 minutes in the refrigerator before it is rolled. The cooked pastry has a crumbly, biscuit-like texture, which is perfect for sweet tarts and fruit flans.

Ready-made shortcrust and sweet shortcrust pastries are available commercially, either fresh or frozen, from most larger supermarkets. These can be used instead of homemade pastry if you prefer.

puff pastry Puff pastry is made up of hundreds of layers of dough interlaced with butter, enabling it to rise in tiny, feather-light layers as it cooks. Making puff pastry can be challenging and is time consuming but the rewards are great. However, there are several brands of ready-made puff pastry available commercially in block form, and these are extremely good. I don't recommend the ready-rolled sheets, which tend to be inferior in quality. Puff pastry is used both as a lid and a pastry case.

flaky pastry Flaky pastry is similar to puff pastry but is quicker to make as the butter is added in small pieces rather than in a block and the dough is only rolled and folded twice. Flaky pastry is used both as a lid and a pastry case.

choux pastry Unlike other types of pastry, choux pastry is a thick batter, which requires piping rather than rolling out. The batter is made in a pan over heat and is beaten to incorporate air. During the second cooking in the oven, the mixture rises, forming a bun with a firm, golden crust and a hollow centre. Once cooled, the bun can be filled with whipped cream or crème patissière. Choux pastry is traditionally used to make èclairs and profiteroles. It cannot be frozen.

successful pastry making

- Make sure the kitchen is as cool as possible.
- Always use chilled butter from the refrigerator and make sure that water is cold or chilled.
- Always sift plain flour before using to help aerate the dough.
- Add liquid to flour gradually so that, if the mixture feels too dry, you can add a little more. If it feels too wet add a little more flour.
- Always work the dough as lightly and as quickly as possible, keeping it as cool as you can.
- Always knead and roll out dough on a lightly floured surface. If the dough is very soft or sticky, roll it out between pieces of baking paper.
- When you roll dough, roll in one direction from the centre outwards rotating it each time. Use a marble surface if possible.
- Never pull or stretch the pastry as you roll it, or the pastry will shrink back during cooking.
- When you line a flan tin roll the dough over the rolling pin and then gently unroll it over the tin, allowing the pastry to overhang the edges. Press lightly into the base and then, using the rolling pin, roll over the top of the tin to remove excess pastry. Prick the base lightly with a fork and chill again according to the recipe.

baking blind Baking blind refers to the process by which a pastry case is baked on its own before the filling is added (to be cooked again or served). Line the chilled pastry case with baking paper and baking beans and bake as specified in the recipe. Always allow the pastry case to cool before you add the filling.

storing pastry Store cooked pastries in airtight containers or in the refrigerator if they are filled with cream. Pastry can be frozen raw in a block or as a raw shell, or pastry cases can be baked blind and then frozen ready for filling.

biscuits Biscuits and cookies are actually the same thing. In America all biscuits are cookies, and the word is derived from *koekge*, a word taken to North America by Dutch settlers. In Britain large, chunky biscuits are sometimes referred to as cookies, and elsewhere both words are used to describe the same things. It's a matter of personal preference.

Biscuits share similarities with both cakes and pastries in the way they are made. They can be creamed, whisked, melted-in or rubbed in. Biscuits are shaped in many ways. Some are rolled out thinly and cut or stamped into shapes. Others are formed into blocks or logs and refrigerated until firm enough to slice. Some are shaped into small balls and flattened into rounds, while softer doughs are dropped a spoonful at a time on to a baking sheet. They can be also be piped directly on to the baking sheet.

Biscuits can be left plain or iced or sandwiched together with soft fillings. They can be flavoured with citrus, spices, extracts, nuts and dried fruit. They can be sweet or savoury, with wafers flavoured with spices, cheese or herbs.

A slice (sometimes called a bar or tray bake) is more substantial than a biscuit. It is cooked in a single batch in a rectangular or square tin and is cut into slices (or squares) when cooled. Slices are a combination of biscuit, cake and even pastry.

Everyone loves a chocolate brownie, and although slices are mainly American inventions there are examples of these delicious snacks from around the world, with Lamingtons from Australia and baklavas from the eastern Mediterranean. The traditional Scottish shortbread is often baked in a rectangular tin and served in fingers.

successful biscuit making

- Weigh and measure ingredients accurately because even small deviations can affect the result.
- Chilled butter should be used straight from the refrigerator. Softened butter should be removed

1 hour before use to soften it just a little. Eggs should be removed from the refrigerator 45 minutes before they are needed.

- Always prepare baking sheets and preheat the oven before you start.
- Make sure the oven shelves are set an equal distance apart if you are cooking more than one baking sheet at a time.
- Because some biscuits spread during cooking, always leave a gap between them to be safe.
- Never put biscuit dough on hot baking sheets. Make sure they are cool first.
- Always cook biscuits for the minimum time given. If they are not cooked, return to the oven and check every minute, because they can brown very quickly.
- Biscuits should always be cooled on a wire rack, unless otherwise indicated. Allow biscuits to cool completely before icing or filling.

storing biscuits
Biscuits keep really well, especially the plainer types. Store them in plastic containers or airtight jars. Slices keep well too and should be stored in airtight containers.

all types of baking

- Always read a recipe through to the end before you begin.
- Measure ingredients accurately with measuring spoons and scales.
- Preheat ovens as indicated in the recipe.
- Pay careful attention to cooking times.

Equipment

You will probably already have all the equipment you need if you do any cooking at all, but the items in the following list are essential.

- Two baking sheets
- Baking tins in various shapes and sizes
- One large wire rack
- Electric hand beaters (great for cakes)
- One large and one small measuring jug
- Measuring spoons (these are essential for all types of baking)
- A range of mixing bowls, from small through to extra large
- An oven thermometer (a must for accuracy)
- Several pastry brushes
- Rolling pin (a wooden pin with flat ends is best)
- At least two sieves
- A timer if your oven doesn't have one already
- Accurate scales (electric are best)
- A food processor and electric mixer are useful if you tend to bake often, but they are not essential

The essential baker

Shortcrust pastry dough

ingredients 200 g (7 oz) plain flour, sifted, ½ teaspoon salt, 100 g (3½ oz) chilled butter, diced, 2–3 tablespoons cold water

method **ONE** Put the flour and salt in a food processor, add the butter and pulse briefly until the mixture resembles fine breadcrumbs. Add the water and process again until the pastry just starts to come together. **TWO** Transfer the dough to a lightly floured surface, knead gently and form into a flat disc. Wrap the dough in clingfilm and chill for 20 minutes. **THREE** Remove the dough from the refrigerator and roll it out on a lightly floured surface according to the recipe.

makes 375 g (12 oz), enough for 1 x 25 cm (10 inch) tart case or 2 x 12 cm (5 inch) tartlet cases

note To make the dough by hand put the flour and salt in a bowl and use your fingertips to rub in the butter until the mixture resembles fine breadcrumbs. Make a well in the centre and gradually work in the water to form a soft dough. Knead gently on a lightly floured surface, shape into a flat disc, wrap and chill as above.

Rich shortcrust pastry dough

ingredients 200 g (7 oz) plain flour, sifted, ½ teaspoon salt, 125 g (4 oz) chilled butter, diced, 1 egg yolk, 2–3 tablespoons cold water

method **ONE** Put the flour and salt in a food processor, add the butter and pulse briefly until the mixture resembles fine breadcrumbs. Add the egg yolk and water and process again until the pastry just starts to come together. **TWO** Transfer the dough to a lightly floured surface, knead gently and form into a flat disc. Wrap the dough in clingfilm and chill for 20 minutes. **THREE** Remove from the refrigerator and roll it out on a lightly floured surface according to the recipe.

makes 375 g (12 oz), enough for 1 x 30 cm (12 inch) tart case or 3 x 12 cm (5 inch) tartlet cases

note To make the dough by hand put the flour and salt in a bowl and use your fingertips to rub in the butter until the mixture resembles fine breadcrumbs. Make a well in the centre and gradually work in the egg yolk and water to form a soft dough. Knead gently on a lightly floured surface, shape into a flat disc, wrap and chill as above.

Sweet shortcrust pastry

ingredients 200 g (7 oz) plain flour, sifted, ½ teaspoon salt, 100 g (3½ oz) chilled unsalted butter, diced, 50 g (2 oz) caster sugar, 2 egg yolks, 2–3 tablespoons cold water

method ONE Put the flour and salt in a food processor, add the butter and sugar and pulse briefly until the mixture resembles fine breadcrumbs. Add the egg yolks and water and process until the pastry just starts to come together. Transfer the dough to a lightly floured surface, knead gently and form into a flat disc. Wrap the dough in clingfilm and chill for 30 minutes. TWO Remove the dough from the refrigerator and roll it out on a lightly floured surface according to the recipe.

makes 400 g (13 oz), enough for 1 x 30 cm (12 inch) tart case or 3 x 12 cm (5 inch) tartlet cases

note To make the dough by hand put the flour and salt in a bowl and use your fingertips to rub in the butter until the mixture resembles fine breadcrumbs. Stir in the sugar. Make a well in the centre and gradually work in the egg yolks and water to form a soft dough. Knead gently on a lightly floured surface, shape into a flat disc, wrap and chill as above.

Puff pastry dough

ingredients 250 g (8 oz) plain flour, sifted, 1 teaspoon salt, 250 g (8 oz) chilled unsalted butter, 1 tablespoon lemon juice, 125 ml (4 fl oz) cold water

method **ONE** Put the flour and salt in a bowl and rub in 25 g (1 oz) of the butter until the mixture resembles fine breadcrumbs. Make a well in the centre of the flour and add the lemon juice and cold water. Gradually work together to form a soft dough. **TWO** Put the remaining butter between 2 sheets of clingfilm. Use a rolling pin to roll the butter out to form a 15 cm (6 inch) square. **THREE** Roll out the dough on a lightly floured surface to a 30 cm (12 inch) square. Put the butter diagonally in the centre of the dough, forming a diamond. Fold the exposed dough over the butter, pressing the seams down to completely enclose the butter. Wrap in clingfilm and chill for 20 minutes. **FOUR** Remove the dough from the refrigerator and roll it out on a lightly floured surface to a 20 x 40 cm (8 x 16 inch) rectangle. Fold the top third down towards the centre of the dough and the bottom third up over the top. Press the edges down with the rolling pin to seal. Wrap and chill for 15 minutes. **FIVE** Remove the dough from the refrigerator and turn it through 90 degrees so that the narrow end is towards you. Roll, fold and chill for a further 15 minutes. Repeat the turning, rolling and folding process a further 3 times. Use the pastry as required.

makes 675 g (1 lb 6 oz)

Flaky pastry dough

ingredients 200 g (7 oz) plain flour, sifted, 1 teaspoon salt, 150 g (5 oz) chilled unsalted butter, diced, 100 ml (3½ fl oz) cold water

method **ONE** Put the flour and salt into a bowl and rub in 25 g (1 oz) of the butter until the mixture resembles fine breadcrumbs. Gradually work in enough water to form a soft dough. Transfer the dough to a lightly floured surface, knead gently and shape into a block. Wrap in clingfilm and chill for 15 minutes. **TWO** Remove the dough from the refrigerator and roll it out on a lightly floured surface to form a 15 x 30 cm (6 x 12 inch) rectangle. Dot half the remaining butter over the top two-thirds of the dough, leaving a 1 cm (½ inch) border. Fold the bottom one-third of dough into the centre and over again to meet the top edge, enclosing the butter. Press the edges together well to seal in the butter. Wrap in clingfilm and chill for 15 minutes. **THREE** Remove the dough from the refrigerator, turn it through 90 degrees so that the narrow end is towards you and roll out as before. Dot over the remaining butter and fold over the dough as before. Press the edges together well to seal in the butter. Wrap in clingfilm and chill for at least 15 minutes or until required.

makes 475 g (15 oz)

Choux pastry dough

ingredients 125 ml (4 fl oz) water, 50 g (2 oz) chilled unsalted butter, 2 eggs, lightly beaten, 65 g (2½ oz) plain flour, sifted, pinch of salt

method **ONE** Put the water and butter in a small saucepan and heat gently until the butter has melted. Bring to the boil, remove the pan from the heat and immediately beat in the flour and salt until evenly combined. **TWO** Return the pan to a gentle heat and cook, stirring with a wooden spoon, until the mixture comes together and starts to leave the sides of the pan. **THREE** Remove from the heat and beat in the eggs with a wooden spoon a little at a time, beating well after each addition until the egg is incorporated and the mixture is smooth and shiny. Use as required.

makes enough for 12 profiteroles

Basic pizza dough

This simple bread dough makes the perfect crust for pizzas, and this recipe is sufficient for 2 medium-sized pizzas.

ingredients 250 g (8 oz) white bread flour, 1 teaspoon fast-acting yeast, 1 teaspoon salt, ½ teaspoon sugar, 150 ml (¼ pint) warm water, 1 tablespoon extra virgin olive oil

method **ONE** Sift the flour into the bowl of a food mixer and stir in the yeast, salt and sugar. Add the water and oil, set the mixer to low and work the ingredients until they just come together. Increase the speed and knead the dough for 8–10 minutes until smooth and elastic. **TWO** Shape the dough into a ball and put it in a lightly oiled bowl. Cover with clingfilm and leave to rise in a warm place for 1 hour until the dough has doubled in size. Transfer the risen dough to a lightly floured surface and knock out the air. Use as required.

makes dough for 2 x 30 cm (12 inch) pizza bases

note To make the dough by hand sift the flour and salt into a bowl. Add the sugar then make a well in the centre and add the frothed yeast, water and oil. Using your hands, gradually work the ingredients together to form a soft dough. Turn out the dough on to a lightly floured surface and knead for 8–10 minutes until it is smooth and elastic. Continue as above.

Pastry cream

Also known as crème patissière, pastry cream is a thickened custard used to fill sweet pastry cases and choux buns.

ingredients 300 ml (½ pint) milk, 1 vanilla pod, split, 3 egg yolks, 50 g (2 oz) caster sugar, 2 tablespoons cornflour, 2 tablespoons plain flour, 15 g (½ oz) unsalted butter

method **ONE** Put the milk in a saucepan and scrape in the seeds from the vanilla pod. Bring the milk slowly to the boil and remove from the heat. **TWO** In a bowl whisk together the egg yolks and sugar and then whisk in the cornflour and flour until the mixture is smooth. **THREE** Whisk in the hot milk and then return the mixture to the pan. Heat gently, stirring constantly until the mixture just starts to boil. Simmer for 1 minute, remove from the heat and whisk in the butter. Cover the surface with clingfilm and set aside to cool completely. Use as required.

makes 350 ml (12 fl oz)

note It is really important to stir the mixture constantly as it cooks so that it thickens but doesn't become lumpy. If this does happen, put the pastry cream in a food processor and process until it is smooth. Always cover the surface of the cream with clingfilm as it cools to prevent a skin forming.

Cakes

Raspberry and coconut friands

Friands are traditional Australian small cakes made in oval tins. They are buttery and rich and great with a cup of tea. Use a muffin tray as an alternative.

ingredients

75 g (3 oz) plain flour, 200 g (7 oz) icing sugar, 125 g (4 oz) ground almonds, 50 g (2 oz) desiccated coconut, grated rind of 1 lemon, 5 egg whites, 175 g (6 oz) unsalted butter, melted, 125 g (4 oz) raspberries

method

ONE Sift the flour and icing sugar into a bowl and stir in the ground almonds, coconut and lemon rind. **TWO** Whisk the egg whites in a separate bowl until they are frothy and fold them into the dry ingredients. Add the melted butter and stir until evenly combined. **THREE** Spoon the mixture into 9 lightly oiled friand tins (or a muffin tray). Top each friand with a few raspberries and bake in a preheated oven, 200°C (400°F), Gas Mark 6, for 18–20 minutes until a skewer inserted into the centre comes out clean. Leave to cool for 5 minutes in the tins and then turn out on to a wire rack to cool completely.

preparation time 10 minutes
cooking time 18–20 minutes

makes 9 cakes

Gingerbread
Rich, moist gingerbread keeps well and should be stored for several days before eating as the flavour develops with time.

ingredients
500 g (1 lb) self-raising flour, 1 tablespoon ground ginger, ½ teaspoon bicarbonate of soda, ½ teaspoon salt, 175 g (6 oz) light soft brown sugar, 175 g (6 oz) unsalted butter, 175 ml (6 fl oz) black treacle, 175 ml (6 fl oz) golden syrup, 300 ml (½ pint) milk, 1 egg, lightly beaten

method
ONE Sift the flour, ginger, bicarbonate of soda and salt into a bowl. Put the sugar, butter, treacle and syrup into a saucepan and heat gently until the butter has melted and the sugar has dissolved. **TWO** Pour the liquid into the dry ingredients together with the milk and egg and beat with a wooden spoon until smooth. **THREE** Transfer the mixture to an oiled and base-lined 20 x 30 cm (8 x 12 inch) baking tin. Bake in a preheated oven, 160°C (325°F), Gas Mark 3, for 1¼ hours or until a skewer inserted into the centre comes out clean. Leave to cool in the tin for 10 minutes and then turn out on to a wire rack to cool. Wrap the cooled cake in foil and store in an airtight container for up to 5 days.

preparation time 10 minutes
cooking time 1¼ hours

serves 24

Chocolate marble cake You can use either a plain ring tin for this cake or the more decorative bundt and kugelhopf tins, if preferred.

ingredients 250 g (8 oz) unsalted butter, softened, 175 g (6 oz) caster sugar, 4 eggs, lightly beaten, 225 g (7½ oz) self-raising flour, 1 teaspoon baking powder, pinch of salt, 50 g (2 oz) ground almonds, 125 g (4 oz) dark chocolate, 125 g (4 oz) white chocolate

method ONE Put the butter, sugar, eggs, flour, baking powder, salt and ground almonds in the bowl of an electric mixer and whisk together until evenly combined. Spoon half of the mixture into a clean bowl. TWO Meanwhile, put the dark and white chocolate into separate bowls and put each one over a pan of gently simmering water (do not allow the base of the bowls to touch the water). Stir until the chocolate has melted. THREE Reserving 2 tablespoons of each melted chocolate for decoration, stir the remaining dark chocolate into half the cake mix and the remaining white chocolate into the remaining cake mix, folding together until evenly combined. Spoon both mixtures alternately into an oiled 23 cm (9 inch) kugelhopf tin and use a skewer to swirl the mixture gently to create a marbled effect. Bake in a preheated oven, 180°C (350°F), Gas Mark 4, for 45–50 minutes until a skewer inserted in the centre comes out clean. Cover the cake with foil if it is getting too browned. FOUR Remove the cake from the oven, leave to cool in the tin for 10 minutes, then turn it out on to a wire rack to cool. FIVE Take the reserved dark and white chocolate and warm each through by immersing the bowls into hot water, stirring until melted. Use teaspoons to drizzle the chocolate over the cake and serve in slices.

preparation time 20 minutes
cooking time 45–50 minutes

serves 8

note To make the cake by hand *see page 39*, folding in all ingredients except the chocolate.

Chocolate truffle cake

This rich dark cake sinks and cracks as it cools giving it a wonderfully truffle-like texture. Serve it whilst still warm with strawberries and cream.

ingredients

250 g (8 oz) plain chocolate, chopped, 125 g (4 oz) unsalted butter, 50 ml (2 fl oz) double cream, 4 eggs, separated, 125 g (4 oz) caster sugar, 2 tablespoons cocoa powder, sifted, icing sugar, to dust **to serve** whipped cream, strawberries

method

ONE Melt the chocolate, butter and cream together in a bowl set over a pan of gently simmering water (do not allow the bowl to touch the water) until melted. Remove from the heat and leave to cool for 5 minutes. **TWO** Whisk the egg yolks with 75 g (3 oz) of the sugar until pale and then stir in the cooled chocolate mixture. **THREE** Whisk the egg whites in a clean bowl until soft peaks form and then whisk in the remaining sugar. Fold into the egg mixture with the sifted cocoa powder until evenly incorporated. **FOUR** Oil and base-line a 23 cm (9 inch) spring-form cake tin and lightly dust all over with a little extra cocoa powder. Pour the cake mix into the prepared tin and bake in a preheated oven, 180°C (350°F), Gas Mark 4, for 35 minutes. Leave to cool in the tin for 10 minutes and turn out on to a serving plate. Dust the cake with icing sugar and serve in wedges with whipped cream and strawberries.

preparation time 15 minutes
cooking time 35 minutes

serves 8

Pear, cardamom and sultana cake This moist fruitcake is made in a loaf tin and served in slices. It is delicious served with a cup of tea.

ingredients 125 g (4 oz) unsalted butter, softened, 125 g (4 oz) light soft brown sugar, 2 eggs, lightly beaten, 250 g (8 oz) self-raising flour, 1 teaspoon ground cardamom, 4 tablespoons milk, 500 g (1 lb) pears, peeled, cored and thinly sliced, 125 g (4 oz) sultanas, 1 tablespoon clear honey

method ONE Using electric beaters, cream the butter and sugar together until pale and light and then gradually beat in the eggs, a little at a time, until incorporated. Sift the flour and ground cardamom together and fold them into the creamed mixture with the milk. TWO Reserve about one-third of the pear slices and roughly chop the rest. Fold the chopped pears into the creamed mixture with the sultanas. Oil and base-line a 1 kg (2 lb) loaf tin with greaseproof paper and spoon the mixture into the tin. Smooth the surface, making a small dip in the centre. THREE Arrange the reserved pear slices down the centre of the cake, pressing them in gently. Bake in a preheated oven, 160°C (325°F), Gas Mark 3, for 1¼–1½ hours or until a skewer, inserted in the centre, comes out clean. Remove the cake from the oven and brush over the clear honey. Leave to cool in the tin for 20 minutes and then transfer to a wire rack to cool completely.

preparation time 20 minutes
cooking time 1¼–1½ hours

serves 12

Whisked sponge with lemon curd

With its light texture this cake is a classic whisked sponge – it provides the perfect base for an array of delicious fillings from lemon curd to soft fruits.

ingredients **6 eggs, 175 g (6 oz) caster sugar, 175 g (6 oz) plain flour, sifted, 50 g (2 oz) unsalted butter, melted, caster sugar, to dust** filling **150 ml (¼ pint) double cream, 6 tablespoons lemon curd**

method **ONE** Put the eggs and sugar in a bowl set over a pan of gently simmering water and, using electric beaters, whisk the eggs for 5 minutes until thickened to the ribbon stage (*see page 12*). **TWO** Remove the bowl from the pan and gently fold in the flour and then the melted butter. Oil and base-line 2 x 20 cm (8 inch) cake tins. Divide the mixture evenly between the cake tins and bake in a preheated oven, 180°C (350°F), Gas Mark 4, for 25–30 minutes until springy to the touch. Cool in the tins for 5 minutes, then turn out on to a wire rack to cool. **THREE** To assemble the cake whip the cream until thick. Spread the lemon curd over one cake, then top with the whipped cream and the second sponge. Dust with caster sugar and serve in wedges.

preparation time 15 minutes
cooking time 25–30 minutes

serves 8

Victoria sandwich A true classic, this buttery sponge cake can be served sandwiched with a little jam or, for a more elaborate occasion, with some whipped cream and fresh raspberries.

ingredients
250 g (8 oz) unsalted butter, softened, 250 g (8 oz) caster sugar, plus extra for serving, 4 eggs, lightly beaten, 250 g (8 oz) self-raising flour, pinch of salt, 1 tablespoon milk, 1 teaspoon vanilla essence, raspberry or strawberry jam, for filling

method
ONE Put all the ingredients into the bowl of an electric mixer, set the mixer to medium and whisk together for 1 minute or until evenly blended. **TWO** Oil and base-line 2 x 20 cm (8 inch) cake tins. Divide the mixture equally between the tins and bake in a preheated oven, 180°C (350°F), Gas Mark 4, for 25–30 minutes or until risen and firm to the touch. Remove from the oven, leave to cool in the tin for 5 minutes and then transfer the sponge cakes to a wire rack to cool. **THREE** Sandwich the sponges together with jam and serve dusted with caster sugar.

variation
For chocolate sponge cake, follow the method above but replace 50 g (2 oz) of the flour with cocoa powder. Bake as normal. Fill the cake with a simple chocolate icing (*see page 80*) and dust with caster sugar.

preparation time 5 minutes
cooking time 25–30 minutes

serves 8

note To make the cake by hand cream the butter and sugar together until pale and light, then beat in the eggs a little at a time until incorporated. Fold in the flour, salt and milk and continue as above.

Apple, Brazil nut and fig muffins

You can make these muffins in classic muffin cases or straight-sided paper cases, whichever you prefer.

ingredients 250 g (8 oz) plain flour, 1½ teaspoons baking powder, ½ teaspoon ground cinnamon, 50 g (2 oz) Brazil nuts, chopped, 175 g (6 oz) granulated sugar, 1 egg, lightly beaten, 300 ml (½ pint) buttermilk, 50 g (2 oz) unsalted butter, melted, 1 apple, peeled, cored and diced, 75 g (3 oz) dried figs, chopped

method **ONE** Sift the flour, baking powder and cinnamon into a bowl and stir in the Brazil nuts and sugar. Beat together the egg, buttermilk and melted butter until blended and stir into the dry ingredients to make a smooth batter. **TWO** Put 8 paper cases on a baking sheet or in a muffin tray. Fold in the apple and figs and spoon the mixture into the paper cases. Bake in a preheated oven, 200°C (400°F), Gas Mark 6, for about 30–35 minutes until risen and golden. Leave to cool on a wire rack and serve the muffins warm.

preparation time 10 minutes
cooking time 30–35 minutes

makes 8 muffins

Banana and walnut spice cake
This cake is made in a bundt tin – an ornate ring tin, which has become very popular in many baking circles. You can use a plain ring tin if preferred.

ingredients 250 g (8 oz) unsalted butter, softened, 250 g (8 oz) light soft brown sugar, 4 eggs, beaten, 250 g (8 oz) self-raising flour, 1½ teaspoons baking powder, 1 teaspoon ground mixed spice, pinch of salt, 3 bananas, peeled and mashed, 65 g (2½ oz) walnuts, toasted and finely chopped, icing sugar, to dust

method ONE Put the butter, sugar and eggs in the bowl of a food mixer and sift in the flour, baking powder, spice and salt. Beat for 1 minute until smooth and then stir in the mashed bananas and the walnuts. TWO Spoon the cake mix into an oiled bundt tin and bake in a preheated oven, 160°C (325°F), Gas Mark 3, for 1–1¼ hours or until a skewer inserted in the centre comes out clean. Leave to cool in the tin for 5 minutes then turn out on to a wire rack to cool. Serve dusted with icing sugar.

preparation time 10 minutes
cooking time 1–1¼ hours

serves 8–10

note If you are making the cake by hand, cream the butter and sugar together in a bowl until pale and light and then gradually beat in the eggs a little at a time until incorporated. Fold in the remaining ingredients and continue as above.

Chocolate and chestnut roulade

Roulades traditionally split and crack when rolled, so don't worry if this happens. Once dusted with icing sugar the finished cake looks lovely.

ingredients

125 g (4 oz) dark chocolate, 5 eggs, separated, 175 g (6 oz) caster sugar, plus extra to sprinkle, 2 tablespoons cocoa powder, sifted, 250 g (8 oz) unsweetened chestnut purée, 4 tablespoons icing sugar, 1 tablespoon brandy, 250 ml (8 fl oz) double cream, icing sugar, to dust

method

ONE Put the chocolate in a bowl set over a saucepan of gently simmering water (do not allow the base of the bowl to touch the water) and stir until it has melted. Cool for 5 minutes. **TWO** Put the egg yolks in a bowl, add the sugar and whisk together for 5 minutes until pale and thickened. Stir in the melted chocolate and cocoa powder. Whisk the egg whites in a clean bowl until stiff and fold into the chocolate mixture until evenly combined. **THREE** Oil and line a 23 x 33 cm (9 x 13 inch) Swiss roll tin. Transfer the mixture to the tin, spreading it well into the corners and smooth the surface with a palette knife. Bake in a preheated oven, 180°C (350°F), Gas Mark 4, for 20 minutes until risen and set. **FOUR** Meanwhile, put a large sheet of baking paper on the work surface and sprinkle it with caster sugar. Remove the roulade from the oven and immediately turn it out on to the sugared paper. Carefully remove the lining paper and cover the roulade with a clean tea towel. Set aside to cool. **FIVE** Put the chestnut purée and icing sugar in a food processor and purée until smooth. Transfer the mixture to a bowl and stir in the brandy. Gently whisk in the cream until light and fluffy. Spread the filling over the roulade, leaving a 1 cm (½ inch) border, and roll it up from one short end to form a log. Serve dusted with icing sugar.

preparation time 20 minutes
cooking time 20 minutes

serves 8

Maple, pecan and white chocolate muffins

Maple syrup adds a lovely caramel flavour to these muffins – I love the way they rise over the top of their paper cases as they bake.

ingredients 300 g (10 oz) self-raising flour, 1 teaspoon baking powder, 125 g (4 oz) soft brown sugar, 1 egg, 50 ml (2 fl oz) maple syrup, 250 ml (8 fl oz) milk, 50 g (2 oz) unsalted butter, melted, 125 g (4 oz) white chocolate, chopped, 75 g (3 oz) pecan nuts, coarsely chopped to decorate chopped pecans, chopped white chocolate

method ONE Sift the flour and baking powder into a bowl and stir in the sugar. Beat together the egg, syrup, milk and melted butter and beat into the dry ingredients until mixed. Fold in the chocolate and pecan nuts. TWO Line 8 holes of a muffin tray with paper cases. Divide the mixture among the paper cases and top with some extra chopped nuts and chocolate. Bake in a preheated oven, 200°C (400°F), Gas Mark 6, for 20–25 minutes until risen and golden. Leave to cool on a wire rack.

preparation time 10 minutes
cooking time 20–25 minutes

makes 8 muffins

Baked cheesecake with passionfruit syrup

Baked cheesecake with passionfruit syrup Once the cheesecake is cooked, switch off the oven and leave the cake to cool with the door ajar. This will prevent the cake from cracking.

ingredients 175 g (6 oz) digestive biscuits, crushed, 75 g (3 oz) unsalted butter, melted, 250 g (8 oz) full-fat ricotta cheese, 250 g (8 oz) cream cheese, 250 g (8 oz) crème fraîche or sour cream, 3 eggs, 125 g (4 oz) caster sugar, grated rind and juice of 1 lemon, 2 tablespoons cornflour passionfruit syrup 100 g (3½ oz) caster sugar, 100 ml (3½ fl oz) water, about 75 ml (3 fl oz) pulp from 6 passionfruit

method ONE Spray-oil a 23 cm (9 inch) spring-form cake tin. Combine the crushed biscuits and butter and spoon the mixture into the prepared tin, spreading it smooth. Chill while you prepare the filling. TWO Put the remaining ingredients in a food processor and process until smooth. Transfer to the prepared tin and bake in a preheated oven, 150°C (300°F), Gas Mark 2, for 1 hour. Turn off the heat but allow the cheesecake to cool completely in the oven. THREE Make the passionfruit syrup. Put the sugar and water in a saucepan and heat gently to dissolve the sugar. Add the passionfruit pulp and bring to the boil. Simmer gently for 10 minutes until reduced slightly and thickened. Leave to cool. Serve the cheesecake in wedges drizzled with the syrup.

preparation time 15 minutes
cooking time 1 hour

serves 8

Strawberry shortcake with elderflower cream

Elderflower syrup complements the flavour of the strawberries perfectly in these delicate biscuit-like small cakes.

ingredients

250 g (8 oz) self-raising flour, 2 teaspoons baking powder, 75 g (3 oz) unsalted butter, diced, 40 g (1½ oz) caster sugar, 1 egg, lightly beaten, 2–3 tablespoons milk, 15 g (½ oz) butter, melted, 250 g (8 oz) strawberries, hulled and sliced, icing sugar, to dust **elderflower cream** 300 ml (½ pint) double cream, 2 tablespoons elderflower syrup

method

ONE Sift the flour and baking powder into the bowl of the food processor and add the butter. Pulse briefly until the mixture resembles fine breadcrumbs. Stir in the sugar. Add the egg and milk and process until the mixture just comes together to form a dough. **TWO** Transfer the dough to a lightly floured surface and roll it out to 1 cm (½ inch) thick. Use a 7 cm (3 inch) round cutter to stamp out 8 rounds. Place the rounds on a large, lightly oiled baking sheet and brush each with a little melted butter. Bake in a preheated oven, 200°C (400°F), Gas Mark 6, for 10–15 minutes until risen and golden. Remove from the oven and transfer to a wire rack to cool. While they are still warm carefully split each cake in half horizontally and return to the wire rack to go cold. **THREE** Make the elderflower cream. Put the cream and elderflower syrup in a bowl and whisk until thickened. Spread the cream over the base of each cake, top with strawberries and the cake lids. Serve dusted with icing sugar.

preparation time 20 minutes
cooking time 10–15 minutes

makes 8 cakes

note If making the dough by hand, sift the flour and baking powder into a bowl, rub in the butter, stir in the sugar and then gradually work in the egg and milk to form a soft dough.

Lemon polenta cake with red wine strawberries

Polenta adds a lovely texture and nutty flavour to this cake, which is best served as a dessert with the rich red wine and strawberry syrup.

ingredients 125 g (4 oz) plain flour, 1½ teaspoons baking powder, 125 g (4 oz) polenta, 3 eggs, plus 2 egg whites, 175 g (6 oz) golden caster sugar, grated rind and juice of 2 lemons, 100 ml (3½ fl oz) vegetable oil, 150 ml (¼ pint) buttermilk **red wine strawberries** 300 ml (½ pint) red wine, 1 vanilla pod, split, 150 g (5 oz) caster sugar, 2 tablespoons balsamic vinegar, 250 g (8 oz) strawberries, hulled

method **ONE** Sift the flour and baking powder into a bowl and stir in the polenta, set aside. **TWO** Using electric beaters, whisk the eggs, egg whites and sugar together for 3–4 minutes until pale and thickened. Stir in the polenta mixture, lemon rind and juice, vegetable oil and buttermilk to form a smooth batter. **THREE** Spray-oil and base-line a 25 cm (10 inch) spring-form cake tin and pour the mixture into the tin. Bake in a preheated oven, 180°C (350°F), Gas Mark 4, for 30 minutes until risen and firm to the touch. Leave to cool in the tin for 10 minutes then turn out on to a wire rack to cool. **FOUR** Meanwhile, prepare the red wine strawberries. Put the wine, vanilla pod and sugar in a saucepan and heat gently to dissolve the sugar. Increase the heat and simmer for 10–15 minutes until reduced and syrupy. Leave to cool and then stir in the balsamic vinegar and strawberries. **FIVE** Cut the cake into slices and serve with the strawberries and their syrup.

preparation time 20 minutes
cooking time 30 minutes

serves 8–10

Walnut and orange cake with kumquats

Raw kumquats are very bitter, but cooking them in sugar syrup sweetens and caramelizes them so they become almost candied.

ingredients 6 eggs, separated, 175 g (6 oz) caster sugar, grated rind of 2 oranges, 250g (8 oz) walnuts, ground, 2 tablespoons poppy seeds kumquat compote 500 g (1 lb) kumquats, 200 ml (7 fl oz) water, juice of 1 orange, 200 g (7 oz) granulated sugar, 1 cinnamon stick, bashed lightly, 2 tablespoons Grand Marnier or brandy

method ONE Make the kumquat compote. Cut the kumquats in half and remove the pips. Heat the water, orange juice, sugar and cinnamon stick together in a saucepan until the sugar has dissolved. Add the kumquats and bring to the boil. Simmer very gently for 35–40 minutes or until the kumquats are tender. Remove from the heat and add the Grand Marnier or brandy. Keep warm. TWO Meanwhile, put the egg yolks, sugar and orange rind in the bowl of an electric mixer and whisk together until pale and thickened, then stir in the walnuts and poppy seeds (the mixture will be very thick at this stage). THREE Whisk the egg whites in a separate bowl until stiff, stir a large spoonful into the cake mix to loosen it and then fold in the rest until evenly incorporated. FOUR Oil and base-line a 24 cm (9½ inch) spring-form cake tin. Transfer the cake mixture to the tin and bake in a preheated oven, 180°C (350°F), Gas Mark 4, for 45–50 minutes until risen and firm to the touch, covering the cake with foil if it starts to brown. FIVE Leave the cake to cool in the tin for 10 minutes then transfer it to a plate. Spike the surface with holes and pour over a few tablespoons of the syrup, allowing the juices to soak well in. Leave to cool completely. Serve the cake in wedges with the kumquats and the remaining syrup.

preparation time 20 minutes
cooking time 45–50 minutes

serves 8

Chocolate and hazelnut meringue gateau

Three discs of meringue are baked at once for this cake, so after 30 minutes, swap the top and bottom sheets around for even cooking.

ingredients 5 eggs, separated, 300 g (10 oz) caster sugar, 1 tablespoon cornflour, 125 g (4 oz) blanched hazelnuts, toasted and finely ground, cocoa powder, to dust filling 250 g (8 oz) dark chocolate, chopped, 200 ml (7 fl oz) double cream chocolate hazelnuts 50 g (2 oz) hazelnuts, 50 g (2 oz) dark chocolate, melted

method ONE Whisk the egg whites until they are stiff and gradually whisk in the sugar, a little at a time, until thick and glossy. Fold in the cornflour and ground hazelnuts until evenly incorporated and transfer the mixture to a large piping bag fitted with a 1 cm (½ inch) plain nozzle. TWO Draw 3 x 23 cm (9 inch) circles on 3 sheets of baking paper. Put them on separate baking sheets. Starting in the centre of each prepared circle, pipe the mixture in a continuous coil, finishing just within the line. Bake in a preheated oven, 150°C (300°F), Gas Mark 2, for 1–1¼ hours until lightly golden and dried out. Remove from the oven and transfer to a wire rack to cool completely. Peel away the baking paper. THREE Make the filling. Put the chocolate and cream in a bowl set over a pan of gently simmering water (do not let the bowl touch the water) and heat, stirring until the chocolate is melted. Cool and then chill for 1 hour until thickened. FOUR Make the chocolate hazelnuts. Using a fork, dip the hazelnuts into the melted chocolate until coated. Leave to set on baking paper. FIVE Beat the chocolate filling until it is light and fluffy and use it to sandwich the meringue layers together. Decorate the gateau with the chocolate hazelnuts and serve dusted with cocoa powder.

preparation time 30 minutes, plus chilling
cooking time 1–1¼ hours

serves 8–10

Mocha cup cakes

The chocolate-coated coffee beans used to decorate these little cup cakes are available from specialist food stores and confectioners.

ingredients

250 ml (8 fl oz) water, 250 g (8 oz) caster sugar, 125 g (4 oz) unsalted butter, 2 tablespoons cocoa powder, sifted, ½ teaspoon bicarbonate of soda, 2 tablespoons coffee granules, 225 g (7½ oz) self-raising flour, 2 eggs, lightly beaten, 12 chocolate-covered coffee beans, to decorate

icing

150 g (5 oz) dark chocolate, diced, 150 g (5 oz) unsalted butter, diced, 2 tablespoons golden syrup

method

ONE Put the water and sugar in a saucepan and heat gently, stirring, until the sugar has dissolved. Stir in the butter, cocoa powder, bicarbonate of soda and coffee granules and bring to the boil, simmer for 5 minutes, remove from the heat and set aside to cool. **TWO** Beat the flour and eggs into the cooled chocolate mixture until smooth. Line a 12-hole muffin tray with paper cases and divide the mixture among the cases. Bake in a preheated oven, 180°C (350°F), Gas Mark 4, for 20 minutes until risen and firm. Cool on a wire rack. **THREE** Make the icing. Put the chocolate, butter and syrup in a bowl set over a pan of gently simmering water (do not let the bowl touch the water) stirring until melted. Remove from the heat and leave to cool to room temperature, then chill until thickened. Spread over the cup cakes, top with a chocolate coffee bean and leave to set.

preparation time 15 minutes, plus cooling

cooking time 20 minutes

makes 12 cakes

Plum crumble cake with cinnamon cream

A lovely almond-flavoured sponge topped with halved plums and a buttery crumble finished off with a dollop of cinnamon crème fraîche.

ingredients 175 g (6 oz) unsalted butter, softened, 175 g (6 oz) caster sugar, 3 eggs, lightly beaten, 225 g (7½ oz) self-raising flour, 1 teaspoon baking powder, 100 g (3½ oz) ground almonds, 6 ripe plums, halved and stoned crumble 25 g (1 oz) plain flour, 25 g (1 oz) rolled oats, 25 g (1 oz) unsalted butter, finely diced, 50 g (2 oz) soft brown sugar, 50 g (2 oz) chopped almonds cinnamon crème fraîche 200 g (7 oz) crème fraîche, 1 tablespoon icing sugar, sifted, 1 teaspoon ground cinnamon

method **ONE** Prepare the crumble. Combine the ingredients in a bowl, rubbing the butter in well, and set aside. **TWO** Using electric beaters cream the butter and sugar together until pale and light and then beat in the eggs a little at a time until creamy. Sift over the flour and baking powder, add the ground almonds and fold into the creamed mixture until evenly combined. **THREE** Oil and base-line a 24 cm (9½ inch) cake tin. Spoon the cake mix into the prepared tin and smooth the surface. Arrange the plums, cut side up, over the top of the cake, pressing them down gently into the mix. Scatter the crumble topping evenly over the plums. **FOUR** Bake in a preheated oven, 180°C (350°F), Gas Mark 4, for 50–60 minutes until the cake is risen. Insert a skewer into the centre of the cake, if it comes out clean the cake is cooked. If not, return to the oven for a further 5 minutes and test again. Remove the cake from the oven, leave to cool in the tin for 15 minutes and then turn out on to a wire rack to go cold. **FIVE** Make the cinnamon crème fraîche. Beat the ingredients together until smooth and chill until required. Serve the cake in wedges with the crème fraîche.

preparation time 25 minutes
cooking time 50–60 minutes

serves 8–10

Christmas fruit cake
Rich fruit cakes keep well, so make this cake up to three months in advance, wrap in several layers of foil and store in an airtight tin. Keep in a cool, dark place.

ingredients
250 g (8 oz) sultanas, 175 g (6 oz) raisins, 175 g (6 oz) dried cranberries, 175 g (6 oz) currants, chopped, grated rind and juice of 1 orange, 3 tablespoons orange juice, 200 ml (7 fl oz) whisky, 250 g (8 oz) unsalted butter, softened, 250 g (8 oz) dark soft brown sugar, 5 eggs, 250 g (8 oz) plain flour, 1 tablespoon baking powder, 1½ tablespoons ground mixed spice, 125 g (4 oz) glacé cherries, chopped, 125 g (4 oz) Brazil nuts, roughly chopped, 125 g (4 oz) blanched almonds, roughly chopped, 50 g (2 oz) chopped mixed peel, 50 g (2 oz) ground almonds, 2 tablespoons thick-cut orange marmalade

method
ONE Put the sultanas, raisins, cranberries, currants, orange rind and juice and half the whisky into a large bowl. Leave to marinate overnight. **TWO** Cream the butter and sugar together until pale and light. Beat in the eggs, one at a time, beating well after each addition, until incorporated, adding 2 tablespoons of flour each time. **THREE** Sift the remaining flour, baking powder and mixed spice together and fold into the creamed mixture, alternately with all the remaining ingredients, except for the whisky. **FOUR** Oil and line a 25 cm (10 inch) cake tin with 2 layers of baking paper. Transfer the cake mixture to the prepared tin, smooth the surface, making a small dip in the centre, and bake in a preheated oven, 160°C (325°F), Gas Mark 3, for 1 hour. Reduce the temperature to 150°C (300°F), Gas Mark 2, and bake for a further 1¼–1½ hours until the cake is cooked and a skewer inserted in the centre comes out clean. **FIVE** Remove the cake from the oven, prick it all over with a skewer and pour over the reserved whisky. Leave to cool in the tin for 30 minutes and transfer to a wire rack to cool completely.

preparation time 30 minutes, plus overnight marinating
cooking time 2¼–2½ hours

serves 20–30

Family chocolate cake

This is based on a recipe my mother cooked for us on many occasions as part of our daily 'high tea'. It's a good everyday chocolate cake for kids and grown-ups alike.

ingredients

125 g (4 oz) caster sugar, 4 eggs, 100 g (3½ oz) self-raising flour, 25 g (1 oz) cocoa powder, 40 g (1½ oz) unsalted butter, melted, 1 teaspoon vanilla extract

icing

350 g (12 oz) dark chocolate, 250 g (8 oz) unsalted butter, 100 g (3½ oz) icing sugar, sifted

method

ONE Put the sugar and eggs into a bowl set over a pan of gently simmering water and, using hand-held beaters, beat the mixture for 5 minutes or until it reaches the ribbon stage (*see page 11*). **TWO** Sift over the flour and cocoa powder and carefully fold into the mixture with the melted butter and vanilla extract until combined. **THREE** Oil and base-line a 20 cm (8 inch) spring-form cake tin. Pour the mixture into the tin and bake in a preheated oven, 180°C (350°F), Gas Mark 4, for 25 minutes until risen and firm to the touch. Remove from the oven and leave to cool in the tin for 5 minutes. Turn out and cool on a wire rack. **FOUR** Make the icing. Melt the chocolate and butter together in a bowl set over a pan of just simmering water (do not allow the bowl to touch the water). Remove from the heat and beat in the icing sugar. Set aside to cool and then chill for 1 hour until thickened. Beat until pale and fluffy. **FIVE** Cut the cake in half and use half the icing to sandwich the halves back together. Use the remaining icing to cover the top and sides of the cake, swirling the mixture with a palette knife. Serve in wedges.

preparation time 20 minutes, plus chilling
cooking time 25 minutes

serves 8

Coffee cake with pistachio praline

Don't worry if the icing mixture starts to curdle just before all the butter is added. Keep going and it will become creamy and smooth.

ingredients

6 eggs, 175 g (6 oz) caster sugar, 175 g (6 oz) plain flour, sifted, 50 g (2 oz) unsalted butter, melted, 2 tablespoons made espresso coffee, cooled **praline** 65 g (2½ oz) shelled pistachio nuts, 125 g (4 oz) granulated sugar, 50 ml (2 fl oz) water **maple syrup icing** 6 egg yolks, 175 g (6 oz) caster sugar, 150 ml (¼ pint) milk, 350 g (12 oz) unsalted butter (at room temperature), diced, 3 tablespoons maple syrup

method

ONE Put the eggs and sugar in a bowl set over a pan of gently simmering water. Whisk the eggs for 5 minutes until thickened. Remove the bowl from the heat and fold in the flour, melted butter and coffee. **TWO** Oil and base-line a 23 cm (9 inch) cake tin. Transfer the mixture to the tin and bake in a preheated oven, 180°C (350°F), Gas Mark 4, for 25–30 minutes. Cool in the tin for 5 minutes then turn out on to a wire rack. Cut the cake into three layers. **THREE** Make the praline. Put the nuts on a baking sheet. Heat the sugar and water in a heavy-based saucepan until the sugar melts. Increase heat and stir with a wooden spoon until the sugar turns light golden. Remove from the heat and pour over the nuts. Once set, break the praline into small pieces and then grind to a rough powder. **FOUR** Make the icing. Beat the egg yolks and sugar together until pale and light. Heat the milk until just boiling, then whisk into the egg mixture. Return to the pan and heat gently, stirring until the mixture coats the back of the spoon. Beat the mixture off the heat for 2–3 minutes and then gradually beat in the butter, a little at a time, until the mixture is thick and glossy. Beat in the maple syrup. **FIVE** Fold half the praline into half the icing and use to sandwich the sponges together. Spread the remaining icing over the top and sides of the cake and sprinkle the reserved praline over the top.

preparation time 40 minutes
cooking time 25–30 minutes

serves 12

Coconut cakes with passionfruit icing

I love making these rich coconut cakes in a mini-loaf tin, but you can use a 12-muffin tray if you prefer.

ingredients

125 g (4 oz) unsalted butter, softened, 150 g (5 oz) caster sugar, 2 eggs, 125 g (4 oz) self-raising flour, 100 g (3½ oz) desiccated coconut, 2 tablespoons milk **icing** 125 g (4 oz) icing sugar, sifted, 1–2 tablespoons passionfruit pulp

method

ONE Put all the ingredients in a food processor and process for 1 minute or until evenly blended. **TWO** Oil and base-line an 8-hole mini-loaf tin. Divide the mixture equally into the tin and bake in a preheated oven, 160°C (325°F), Gas Mark 3, for 30–35 minutes until risen and firm to the touch. Remove from the oven, leave to cool in the tin for 5 minutes and then transfer the cakes to a wire rack to cool. **THREE** Make the icing. Beat the ingredients together until smooth. Put the cakes, still on the wire rack, over a large plate and pour over the passionfruit icing, allowing it to drizzle down the sides of the cakes. Leave to set.

preparation time 10 minutes
cooking time 30–35 minutes

makes 8 cakes

note To make the cakes by hand cream the butter and sugar together in a bowl until pale and light, then gradually beat in the eggs, a little at a time, until incorporated. Fold in the flour, coconut and milk and continue as above.

Biscuits

Classic shortbread

This classic Scottish butter biscuit has a rich history that predates Elizabethan times. It was traditionally baked at Christmas and New Year.

ingredients 250 g (8 oz) unsalted butter, softened, 125 g (4 oz) caster sugar, plus extra for dusting, 250 g (8 oz) plain flour, 125 g (4 oz) rice flour, pinch of salt

method **ONE** Put the butter and sugar in a food processor and process until pale and creamy. Sift in the flour, rice flour and salt and process briefly until the ingredients just come together. Transfer to the work surface and knead gently to form a soft dough. Shape into a disc, wrap in clingfilm and chill for 30 minutes. **TWO** Divide the dough in half and roll each piece out on a lightly floured surface to form 2 x 20 cm (8 inch) rounds. Transfer them to 2 lightly oiled baking sheets. Score each piece with a sharp knife, marking it into 8 equal wedges, prick with a fork and use your fingers to flute the edges. **THREE** Sprinkle over a little caster sugar and bake in a preheated oven, 190°C (375°F), Gas Mark 5, for 18–20 minutes until golden. Remove from the oven and, while still hot, cut into wedges through the score marks. Leave to cool on the baking sheet for 5 minutes then transfer to a wire rack to cool. Store in an airtight tin.

preparation time 15 minutes, plus chilling
cooking time 18–20 minutes

makes 16 wedges

note If you are making by hand, cream the butter and sugar together then stir in the remaining ingredients and work together to form a soft dough. Continue as above.

Chocolate chip cookies with ginger

Biscuits tend to be either crisp or chewy – a good choc chip cookie is both. Here the flavour is enhanced with a touch of ginger.

ingredients

100 g (3½ oz) unsalted butter, softened, 100 g (3½ oz) caster sugar, 100 g (3½ oz) light soft brown sugar, 2 eggs, lightly beaten, 200 g (7 oz) self-raising flour, 100 g (3½ oz) chocolate chips, 50 g (2 oz) crystallized ginger, finely chopped

method

ONE Put the butter and sugar in a bowl and, using electric beaters, beat together until light and fluffy. Gradually beat in the eggs, a little at a time, beating well after each addition until the mixture becomes creamy. Stir in the flour and fold in the chocolate chips and ginger to make a soft, sticky dough. **TWO** Drop teaspoonfuls of the mixture, spaced well apart on to 2 lightly oiled baking sheets and bake in a preheated oven, 190°C (375°F), Gas Mark 5, for 10–12 minutes until lightly golden. Leave to cool for 2 minutes on the baking sheets, then use a palette knife to transfer the cookies to a wire rack to cool. Repeat with the remaining dough to make 40 cookies.

preparation time 10 minutes
cooking time 10–12 minutes

makes 40 cookies

Chocolate butter biscuits

Butter biscuits are simple yet delicious and often form the base for iced biscuits. They are also used to make mint chocolate sandwich biscuits (*see page 68*).

ingredients
250 g (8 oz) plain flour, 25 g (1 oz) cocoa powder, pinch of salt, 200 g (7 oz) chilled unsalted butter, diced, 100 g (3½ oz) icing sugar, 2 egg yolks, 1 teaspoon vanilla extract

method
ONE Sift the flour, cocoa powder and salt into a food processor, add the butter and process until the mixture resembles fine breadcrumbs. Add the sugar and pulse briefly, then add the egg yolks and vanilla and process until the mixture just starts to come together. Transfer the dough to a work surface and shape into a disc. Wrap in clingfilm and chill for 30 minutes. **TWO** Roll out the dough on a lightly floured surface to 5 mm (¼ inch) thick. **THREE** Use a 7 cm (3 inch) cookie cutter to stamp out rounds and put them on 3 large, lightly oiled baking sheets. Bake in a preheated oven, 200°C (400°F), Gas Mark 6, for 8–10 minutes until lightly golden around the edges. Leave to cool for 5 minutes on the baking sheets and then transfer to a wire rack to cool.

preparation time 10 minutes, plus chilling
cooking time 8–10 minutes

makes 36 biscuits

note For plain biscuits increase flour to 275 g (9 oz) and omit the cocoa powder.

Peanut butter cookies Chunky, nutty and totally addictive, these are a great hit with the kids, but make sure you set some aside for the grown-ups.

ingredients 125 g (4 oz) unsalted butter, softened, 150 g (5 oz) soft brown sugar, 125 g (4 oz) chunky peanut butter, 1 egg, lightly beaten, 150 g (5 oz) plain white flour, ½ teaspoon baking powder, 125 g (4 oz) unsalted peanuts

method **ONE** Put the butter and sugar in a bowl and, using electric beaters, beat together until pale and fluffy. Add the peanut butter, egg, flour and baking powder and stir together until combined. Stir in the peanuts. **TWO** Take large teaspoonfuls of the mixture and drop them on to 3 large, lightly oiled baking sheets, leaving a good 5 cm (2 inch) gap between them for spreading. Flatten them slightly and bake in a preheated oven, 190°C (375°F), Gas Mark 5, for 12 minutes until golden around the edges. Leave to cool on the baking sheets for 2 minutes, then transfer to a wire rack to go cold.

preparation time 10 minutes
cooking time 12 minutes

makes 32 cookies

note To make peanut butter and chocolate chip cookies replace half the peanuts with milk chocolate chips and cook as above.

Dunking jacks I like to call these ginger snaps dunking jacks because they taste even better when dunked in a hot cup of tea!

ingredients
375 g (12 oz) self-raising flour, 1 tablespoon ground ginger, 1 teaspoon bicarbonate of soda, pinch of salt, 200 g (7 oz) granulated sugar, plus extra for dusting, 125 g (4 oz) unsalted butter, 4 tablespoons black treacle, 1 tablespoon milk, 1 egg, beaten

method
ONE Sift the flour, ginger, bicarbonate of soda and salt into a bowl and stir in the sugar. Put the butter and treacle in a saucepan and heat gently until the butter is melted, remove from the heat and leave to cool for 15 minutes. **TWO** Beat the cooled butter mixture into the dry ingredients with the milk and egg and mix together until evenly combined, then knead briefly until smooth. **THREE** Take 15 g (½ oz) pieces of dough and roll them into balls. Flatten them into 5 cm (2 inch) discs and place them, slightly apart, on 2 large, lightly oiled baking sheets. **FOUR** Sprinkle the biscuits with a little granulated sugar and bake in a preheated oven, 180°C (350°F), Gas Mark 4, for 13–15 minutes until evenly browned. Leave to cool on the baking sheets for 2 minutes then transfer to a wire rack to cool. Repeat with the remaining dough to make 40–44 biscuits.

preparation time 15 minutes
cooking time 13–15 minutes

makes 40–44 biscuits

Chocolate kisses

Two small discs of gooey chocolate macaroons 'kiss' each other with the help of a little chocolate filling. Serve as petit fours with coffee.

ingredients 2 large egg whites, ¼ teaspoon cream of tartar, 225 g (7½ oz) caster sugar, 4 tablespoons cocoa powder, sifted, 150 g (5 oz) ground almonds, 1 teaspoon almond extract, espresso coffee, to serve **icing** 100 g (3½ oz) dark chocolate, chopped, 125 ml (4 fl oz) double cream

method **ONE** Whisk the egg whites and cream of tartar in a clean bowl until stiff, then gradually whisk in the sugar, 1 tablespoon at a time, until the mixture thickens. Fold in the cocoa powder, ground almonds and almond extract with a metal spoon until evenly combined. **TWO** Spoon the mixture into a piping bag fitted with a large star nozzle and pipe 2.5 cm (1 inch) rosettes on to 2 large, lined baking sheets (you should have about 40–50 rosettes, depending on the size). **THREE** Bake in a preheated oven, 150°C (300°F), Gas Mark 2, for 15 minutes until the biscuits are just set. Remove from the oven and leave to cool completely on the baking sheets. **FOUR** Make the icing. Put the chocolate and cream in a bowl set over a pan of gently simmering water (do not allow the bowl to touch the water). Heat gently, stirring until the chocolate is melted. Cool and then chill for 30 minutes. Whip the chocolate mixture until thick and fluffy and use to sandwich the biscuits together to make kisses. Serve with espresso coffee.

preparation time 15 minutes, plus chilling
cooking time 15 minutes

makes about 25 kisses

Mint chocolate sandwiches

Two layers of chocolate butter biscuits are sandwiched together with peppermint icing. The biscuits are then dipped in melted chocolate – yum.

ingredients 1 quantity chocolate butter biscuit dough (*see page 63*) filling 65 g (2½ oz) unsalted butter, softened, 150 g (5 oz) icing sugar, sifted, 1 teaspoon peppermint essence icing 250 g (8 oz) dark chocolate

method **ONE** Make up the biscuit dough according to the recipe on page 63. Roll out the dough on a lightly floured surface until it is 3 mm (⅛ inch) thick. Use a 5 cm (2 inch) plain cookie cutter to stamp out rounds. Put them on 3 large, oiled baking sheets and bake in a preheated oven, 200°C (400°F), Gas Mark 6, for 10 minutes until starting to brown around the edges. Leave to cool on a wire rack. **TWO** Make the filling. Put the butter, icing sugar and peppermint essence in a bowl and, using electric beaters, beat together until smooth. Use it to sandwich the biscuits together. **THREE** Make the icing. Put the chocolate in a bowl set over a pan of gently simmering water (do not allow the bowl to touch the water) and stir until melted. Put the biscuits, one at a time on a fork, dip each one into the melted chocolate and put it on a sheet of baking paper to set. Repeat with the remaining biscuits.

preparation time 15 minutes
cooking time 10 minutes

makes 24–28 biscuits

Almond thins

A meringue-like mixture combined with flour and almonds is twice baked to make these delicate biscuits – ideal with creamy desserts and mousses.

ingredients

3 egg whites, 100g (3½ oz) caster sugar, ½ teaspoon almond essence, 100 g (3½ oz) plain flour, 100 g (3½ oz) blanched almonds

method

ONE Using electric beaters, whisk the egg whites in a bowl until stiff and then whisk in the sugar and almond essence. Sift over the flour and fold into the mixture until really smooth, then fold in the almonds. **TWO** Lightly oil and line a 1 kg (2 lb) loaf tin. Spoon the mixture into the tin and bake in a preheated oven, 180°C (350°F), Gas Mark 4, for 25 minutes until the mixture is risen and golden. Remove from the oven, leave to cool for 5 minutes and then turn out on a wire rack to cool. Reduce the temperature to 140°C (275°F), Gas Mark 1. **THREE** Remove the paper and use a sharp knife to cut the block into wafer-thin slices. Put the slices on 2 large, oiled and lined baking sheets and bake for 15-20 minutes until lightly golden. Cool on a wire rack.

preparation time 20 minutes
cooking time 40–45 minutes

makes 45–50 biscuits

Mother's flapjacks

My mother always uses half margarine and half white vegetable fat to make flapjacks and this is her recipe – they are the best I've ever eaten.

ingredients

100 g (3½ oz) margarine, 100 g (3½ oz) white vegetable fat, 100 g (3½ oz) demerara sugar, 4 tablespoons golden syrup, 350 g (12 oz) rolled oats

method

ONE Put the margarine, fat, sugar and golden syrup in a saucepan and heat gently, stirring, until the margarine and fat are melted and the sugar has dissolved. Remove from the heat and stir in the oats until evenly coated. **TWO** Oil and base-line a 23 x 33 cm (9 x 13 inch) Swiss roll tin. Transfer the mixture to the tin and spread it flat. Bake in a preheated oven, 160°C (325°F), Gas Mark 3, for 35 minutes until the mixture is deep golden all over. Remove from the oven and immediately score the flapjacks into 16 fingers. Leave to cool in the tin, then cut into fingers.

preparation time 10 minutes
cooking time 35 minutes

makes 16 fingers

note Butter can be used instead of margarine, if preferred.

Jammy dodgers

These childhood favourites are also known as thumbprint cookies because a small indentation is made in the biscuit dough and filled with jam before baking.

ingredients

175 g (6 oz) unsalted butter, softened, 250 g (8 oz) caster sugar, 1 egg, lightly beaten, 1 teaspoon almond extract, 250 g (8 oz) plain flour, ½ teaspoon baking powder, 125 g (4 oz) ground almonds, 100 g (3½ oz) raspberry jam

method

ONE Put the butter and sugar in a bowl and, using electric beaters, beat together until light and fluffy. Beat in the egg and almond extract until combined. Sift in the flour and baking powder and use a wooden spoon to stir into the creamed mixture with the ground almonds to form a soft dough. **TWO** Break off 15 g (½ oz) pieces of dough, shape them into balls and flatten them slightly to form 4 cm (1½ inch) discs. Transfer them to 2 large, lightly oiled baking sheets, spacing them well apart, and make an indentation in the centre of each one with your thumb. **THREE** Spoon ¼ teaspoon of jam into the hollow centres and bake in a preheated oven, 180°C (350°F), Gas Mark 4, for 10–12 minutes or until lightly golden. Leave to cool for 5 minutes on the baking sheets and then cool on a wire rack. Repeat with the remaining dough to make 48 biscuits.

preparation time 10 minutes
cooking time 10–12 minutes

makes 48 biscuits

note Jammy dodgers are best eaten on the day they are baked.

Double chocolate brownies

Double chocolate brownies A good brownie should be gooey underneath with a sugary crust – when cooked they should still feel soft in the centre, so be careful not to overcook them.

ingredients 275 g (9 oz) dark chocolate, 250 g (8 oz) unsalted butter, 3 eggs, 175 g (6 oz) caster sugar, 50 ml (2 fl oz) maple syrup, 100 g (3½ oz) self-raising flour, pinch of salt, 100 g (3½ oz) walnuts, toasted and chopped, 125 g (4 oz) white chocolate, chopped

method **ONE** Melt the dark chocolate and butter together in a bowl set over a pan of gently simmering water (do not allow the bowl to touch the water), stirring until melted. **TWO** Using electric beaters, whisk the eggs with the sugar and maple syrup until pale and light and then stir in the melted chocolate mixture, and the flour, salt and walnuts. **THREE** Oil and line a 20 x 30 cm (8 x 12 inch) baking tin, allowing the paper to overhang the edges of the tin. Spoon the mixture into the tin and scatter the white chocolate over the surface. Bake in a preheated oven, 190°C (375°F), Gas Mark 5, for 35–40 minutes until the top sets but the cake mix still feels soft underneath. Cover the tin loosely with foil if the surface begins to brown too much. Leave to cool in the tin and serve cut into squares.

preparation time 15 minutes
cooking time 35–40 minutes

serves 12

Macadamia, fig and ginger cantuccini

Cantuccini are Italian twice-baked biscuits, traditionally served as a dessert with a glass of Vin Santo (dessert wine).

ingredients 2 eggs, 125 g (4 oz) caster sugar, 250 g (8 oz) plain white flour, 1 teaspoon baking powder, grated rind of 1 lemon, 100 g (3½ oz) macadamia nuts, toasted and chopped, 75 g (3 oz) dried figs, finely chopped, 25 g (1 oz) crystallized ginger, finely chopped

method ONE Put the eggs and sugar in a bowl and, using electric beaters, beat together for 5 minutes until pale and thick. Sift in the flour and baking powder and stir into the egg mixture with the remaining ingredients to form a soft, slightly sticky dough. TWO Transfer half of the dough to a well-floured surface and roll into a 8 x 30 cm (3 x 12 inch) flattened log. Transfer to 1 large, lightly oiled baking sheet. Bake in a preheated oven, 180°C (350°F), Gas Mark 4, for 30 minutes. Remove from the oven and reduce the temperature to 150°C (300°F), Gas Mark 2. THREE Use a serrated knife to cut the dough diagonally into slices 1 cm (½ inch) thick and lay them flat on the baking sheet. Bake for a further 20–25 minutes until golden. Cool on a wire rack. Repeat with the remaining dough to make 22 biscuits.

preparation time 15 minutes
cooking time 50–55 minutes

makes 22 biscuits

Florentines
These delicate lacy biscuits make a lovely Christmas gift. Arrange them in a box separated by small squares of baking paper and store in the refrigerator for up to 3 days.

ingredients
150 g (5 oz) unsalted butter, 175 g (6 oz) caster sugar, 4 tablespoons double cream, 75 g (3 oz) chopped mixed peel, 50 g (2 oz) glacé cherries, chopped, 50 g (2 oz) flaked almonds, 40 g (1½ oz) dried cranberries, 25 g (1 oz) pine nuts, 50 g (2 oz) plain flour, 150 g (5 oz) dark chocolate, 150 g (5 oz) white chocolate

method
ONE Put the butter and sugar in a saucepan and heat gently until the butter is melted. Increase the heat and bring the mixture to the boil. Immediately remove the saucepan from the heat, add the cream, mixed peel, cherries, almonds, cranberries, pine nuts and flour and stir well until evenly combined. **TWO** Drop 12 heaped teaspoonfuls of the mixture on to 2 large, lightly oiled baking sheets lined with baking paper, leaving a 5 cm (2 inch) gap for spreading. Bake in a preheated oven, 180°C (350°F), Gas Mark 4, for 7 minutes. Remove the baking sheets from the oven and using a 7 cm (3 inch) cookie cutter carefully drag the edges of the biscuits into neat rounds so that they are about 5 cm (2 inches) across. Bake for a further 3–4 minutes until golden around the edges. Remove from the oven and leave for 2 minutes. Use a palette knife to transfer the biscuits to baking paper and leave to cool. Repeat with the remaining mixture. **THREE** Melt the dark chocolate and white chocolate in separate bowls set over gently simmering water (do not allow the bases of the bowls to touch the water), stirring until the chocolate is smooth. Spoon the melted chocolate into separate paper icing bags and drizzle back and forth over the biscuits. Leave to set.

preparation time 30 minutes
cooking time 40 minutes

makes 48 biscuits

Lemon biscuits

Lemon biscuits I love these crisp little biscuits with a cup of tea in the afternoon. You can also make them with grated orange rind instead of lemon if you prefer.

ingredients

250 g (8 oz) unsalted butter, softened, 100 g (3½ oz) caster sugar, grated rind of 2 lemons, 1 tablespoon lemon juice, 300 g (10 oz) self-raising flour

method

ONE Put the butter, sugar, lemon rind and juice in a bowl and, using electric beaters, beat together until pale and light. Sift in the flour and continue beating to form a stiff dough. **TWO** Roll 15 g (½ oz) pieces of dough into balls and flatten them into 5 cm (2 inch) discs. Score the surface of each one with the back of fork and put them on 3 large, lightly oiled baking sheets. Bake in a preheated oven, 180°C (350°F), Gas Mark 4, for 12–15 minutes until lightly golden. Leave to cool for 5 minutes on the sheets and transfer to a wire rack until cold.

preparation time 10 minutes
cooking time 12–15 minutes

makes 40 biscuits

Pistachio, lemon and honey baklava
Baklava is made from layers of filo pastry, nuts, sugar and spices, drizzled with syrup. The resulting sweetmeat is wonderfully sticky and sweet.

ingredients
175 g (6 oz) shelled pistachio nuts, 125 g (4 oz) blanched almonds, 1 teaspoon ground cinnamon, ½ teaspoon ground mixed spice, 2 tablespoons caster sugar, 12 sheets filo pastry, 125 g (4 oz) unsalted butter, melted **lemon and honey syrup** grated rind and juice of 2 lemons, 250 g (8 oz) clear honey, 150 ml (¼ pint) water

method
ONE Put the pistachio nuts, almonds and spices in a food processor and pulse briefly until the nuts are coarsely ground. Stir in the sugar. **TWO** Lightly oil a 20 x 30 cm (8 x 12 inch) cake tin. Cut the sheets of filo pastry in half crossways so that they are about the same size as the tin. Brush 1 sheet with melted butter and press it into the tin. Continue to brush and layer the sheets until half remain. Scatter over the nut mixture and then top with the remaining pastry, brushing each sheet with melted butter as you go. **THREE** Use a sharp knife to score a diamond pattern into the pastry, cutting down to the base. Drizzle over any remaining butter and bake in a preheated oven, 180°C (350°F), Gas Mark 4, for 20 minutes. Reduce the temperature to 160°C (325°F), Gas Mark 3, and bake for a further 20–25 minutes until the pastry is crisp and golden. **FOUR** Meanwhile, make the syrup. Put the lemon rind, juice, honey and water in a saucepan and heat gently until boiling. Simmer for 5 minutes and remove from heat. Pour the hot syrup over the baklava and leave to cool.

preparation time 30 minutes
cooking time 40–45 minutes

serves 6–8

Lamingtons

Lamingtons are to Australians what the chocolate brownie is to Americans – cubes of sponge cake are coated in chocolate icing and then rolled in desiccated coconut to finish.

ingredients 125 g (4 oz) unsalted butter, softened, 125 g (4 oz) caster sugar, 2 eggs, lightly beaten, 250 g (8 oz) self-raising flour, sifted, pinch of salt, 4 tablespoons milk, 1 teaspoon vanilla extract **icing** 400 g (13 oz) icing sugar, 100 g (3½ oz) cocoa powder, 150–175 ml (5–6 fl oz) boiling water, 200 g (7 oz) desiccated coconut

method **ONE** Put all the cake ingredients in a food processor and process until smooth. Oil and base-line a 18 x 25 cm (7 x 10 inch) cake tin and transfer the mixture to the prepared tin. Smooth the surface with a palette knife and bake in a preheated oven, 190°C (375°F), Gas Mark 5, for 25–30 minutes until risen and firm to the touch. Leave to cool in the tin for 5 minutes and then turn out on to a wire rack to cool. Leave out overnight. **TWO** Make the icing. Sift the icing sugar and cocoa powder into a bowl, make a well in the centre and beat in the boiling water to make a smooth icing with a pouring consistency. **THREE** Cut the cooled cake into 24 squares. Use 2 forks to dip each cake into the icing and then immediately coat with the coconut. Leave to set on baking paper.

preparation time 20 minutes, plus standing overnight
cooking time 25–30 minutes

makes 24 cakes

note If you are making the cake batter by hand beat the butter and sugar together until pale and light. Then beat in the eggs, a little at a time, until incorporated. Sift in the flour and salt and fold into the creamed mixture with the milk and vanilla. Continue as above.

Chocolate cheesecake slice

This is another delicious and wickedly indulgent treat that is best cut into fingers. Any favourite chocolate biscuits can be used for the base.

ingredients

250 g (8 oz) chocolate biscuits, 100 g (3½ oz) unsalted butter, melted, 50 g (2 oz) dark chocolate, 500 g (1 lb) cream cheese, 150 ml (¼ pint) sour cream, 3 eggs, 125 g (4 oz) caster sugar, 1 teaspoon vanilla extract

method

ONE Put the chocolate biscuits in a food processor and process until smooth, then stir into the melted butter until evenly combined. Lightly oil and line a 18 x 25 cm (7 x 10 inch) cake tin with baking paper, allowing the paper to overhang the edges. Spoon the mixture into the prepared tin and spread flat. Chill while preparing the topping. **TWO** Put the chocolate in a bowl set over a pan of gently simmering water (do not let the bowl touch the water) and stir until it has melted. Keep warm. **THREE** Put the cream cheese, cream, eggs, sugar and vanilla extract in a clean bowl and, using electric beaters, beat together until smooth. Pour into the tin and drizzle over the melted chocolate, using a skewer to create a swirling pattern over the creamed mixture. **FOUR** Bake in a preheated oven, 150°C (300°F), Gas Mark 2, for 50–60 minutes until the mixture is firm, remove from the oven and leave to cool. Chill for 1 hour, then carefully remove the cheesecake from the tin and cut it into fingers.

preparation time 20 minutes
cooking time 50–60 minutes

serves 12–16

Olive oil wafers
Make sure you roll the dough thinly so the wafers become crisp and light after baking. Serve with goats' cheese or camembert.

ingredients 250 g (8 oz) plain flour, 1 teaspoon salt, 1 teaspoon baking powder, 1 tablespoon chopped fresh rosemary, 125 ml (4 fl oz) water, 4 tablespoons extra virgin olive oil

method **ONE** Sift the flour, salt and baking powder into a food processor and stir in the rosemary. Add the water and oil and process until the ingredients just come together. Transfer to a lightly floured surface and knead the dough gently until it is smooth. Wrap in clingfilm and chill for 30 minutes. **TWO** Divide the dough into 8 equal pieces and roll them out on a lightly floured surface to a long, thin oval (as long as your baking sheet) and about 12 cm (5 inch) across. Transfer 2 to 2 large, lightly oiled baking sheets and bake in a preheated oven, 190°C (375°F), Gas Mark 5, for 12–15 minutes until evenly golden. Transfer to a wire rack to cool. Repeat with the remaining dough. The biscuits will keep, stored in an airtight container, for up to 7 days.

preparation time 10 minutes, plus chilling
cooking time 12–15 minutes

makes 8 large wafers

note To make the dough by hand sift the flour, salt and baking powder into a bowl and stir in the rosemary. Make a well in the centre, add the water and oil and work the ingredients together to form a soft dough. Continue as above.

Oatcakes

Because these small savoury biscuits are made with melted fat and hot water, it is important to work quickly – as the dough cools it becomes harder to work.

ingredients 350 g (12 oz) medium oatmeal, plus extra for kneading, 125 g (4 oz) oat bran, ½ teaspoon bicarbonate of soda, ½ teaspoon salt, 250 ml (8 fl oz) boiling water, 50 g (2 oz) butter, melted

method **ONE** Combine the oatmeal, oat bran, bicarbonate of soda and salt in a bowl. Make a well in the centre and, using a wooden spoon, stir in the water and melted butter to form a slightly sticky dough. **TWO** Transfer the dough to a lightly floured surface and knead gently until smooth. Roll out the dough until it is about 3 mm (⅛ inch) thick. Using a 7 cm (2½ inch) pastry cutter, stamp out 24 rounds, re-rolling as necessary. **THREE** Transfer the biscuits to 2 large, lightly oiled baking sheets and bake in a preheated oven, 200°C (400°F), Gas Mark 6, for 18–20 minutes until lightly browned. Leave to cool on the baking sheets for 5 minutes then transfer to a wire rack to cool.

preparation time 10 minutes
cooking time 18–20 minutes

makes 24 oatcakes

Caramel pine nut slice
This buttery shortbread biscuit with a layer of rich caramel is topped with dark chocolate for the ultimate sweet indulgence.

ingredients 125 g (4 oz) unsalted butter, softened , 65 g (2½ oz) caster sugar, plus extra for dusting , 125 g (4 oz) plain flour , 65 g (2½ oz) rice flour , pinch of salt , 200 g (7 oz) dark chocolate pine nut caramel 50 g (2 oz) unsalted butter , 50 g (2 oz) soft brown sugar , 395 g (12¾ oz) can sweetened condensed milk , 50 g (2 oz) pine nuts

method **ONE** Put the butter and sugar in a bowl and, using electric beaters, beat together until pale and light. Sift in the flour, rice flour and salt and work the ingredients together to form a soft dough. Shape the dough into a flat disc, wrap in clingfilm and chill for 30 minutes. **TWO** Oil and line a 20 cm (8 inch) square baking tin with baking paper, allowing the paper to overhang the sides of the tin. Roll out the dough on a lightly floured surface and press into the prepared tin, smoothing it as flat as possible. Bake in a preheated oven, 190°C (375°F), Gas Mark 5, for 20–25 minutes until golden. Remove from the oven and leave to cool. **THREE** Make the pine nut caramel. Put the butter, sugar and condensed milk in a saucepan and heat gently, stirring constantly until the butter has melted and the sugar has completely dissolved. Increase the heat and bring to the boil, whisking constantly for up to 5 minutes until the mixture thickens. Remove from the heat, stir in the pine nuts and pour the mixture over the shortbread layer. Leave until set. Chill for 2 hours until really firm. **FOUR** Put the chocolate in a bowl set over a pan of gently simmering water (do not let the bowl touch the water), stirring until melted. Pour over the caramel layer and spread flat with a palette knife. Leave to set, remove from the tin and cut the mixture into fingers.

preparation time 20 minutes, plus chilling
cooking time 20–25 minutes

serves 12

Pastries

Pecan, maple syrup and chocolate tart Here cocoa powder replaces some of the plain flour to make a chocolate shortcrust pastry.

ingredients 175 g (6 oz) plain flour, sifted, 25 g (1 oz) cocoa powder, sifted, ½ teaspoon salt, 100 g (3½ oz) chilled butter, diced, 1 egg, lightly beaten, 2–3 teaspoons cold water, double cream, to serve filling 125 g (4 oz) unsalted butter, softened, 125 g (4 oz) light soft brown sugar, 2 eggs, beaten, 4 tablespoons plain flour, pinch of salt, 175 ml (6 fl oz) maple syrup, 175 g (6 oz) pecan nuts, toasted, 100 g (3½ oz) pine nuts, lightly toasted, 50 g (2 oz) dark chocolate, chopped

method ONE Make the pastry. Put the flour, cocoa powder and salt in a food processor, add the butter and pulse briefly until the mixture resembles fine breadcrumbs. Add the egg and water and process again until the pastry just starts to come together. Transfer the dough to a lightly floured surface, knead gently and form into a flat disc. Wrap the dough in clingfilm and chill for 30 minutes. TWO Roll out the dough on a lightly floured surface and use it to line a 23 cm (9 inch) square flan tin, prick the base and chill for a further 20 minutes. Line the pastry case with baking paper and baking beans and bake in a preheated oven, 200°C (400°F), Gas Mark 6, for 15 minutes. Remove the paper and beans and bake for a further 12–15 minutes or until crisp and golden. Leave to cool. Reduce the temperature to 180°C (350°F), Gas Mark 4. THREE Prepare the filling. Cream the butter and sugar together until pale and light and then gradually beat in the eggs, a little at a time, adding the flour and salt as you go until everything is evenly combined. Stir in the syrup (the mixture may appear to curdle at this stage, but keep going), nuts and chocolate and spoon the mixture into the pastry case. Bake for 40–45 minutes until golden and just firm in the centre. Remove from the oven and leave to cool. Serve warm with double cream.

preparation time 20 minutes, plus chilling
cooking time 67–75 minutes

serves 8

Fresh strawberry tart
The lemon juice in the pastry ensures a firmer pastry case, ideal for this type of pastry that is not eaten straight away. It prevents the pastry becoming soggy.

ingredients
200 g (7 oz) plain flour, ½ teaspoon salt, 125 g (4 oz) chilled butter, diced, 1 egg yolk, ¼ teaspoon lemon juice, 2–3 tablespoons cold water **filling** 1 quantity pastry cream (*see page 25*), 350 g (12 oz) strawberries, 4 tablespoons strawberry jam, 1 teaspoon water

method
ONE Sift the flour and salt into the food processor, add the butter and process until the mixture resembles fine breadcrumbs. Add the egg yolk, lemon juice and water and process until the mixture just comes together. Transfer the dough to a lightly floured surface, knead gently and form into a flat disc. Wrap the dough in clingfilm and chill for 20 minutes. **TWO** Roll out the pastry on a lightly floured surface. Line the pastry case with baking paper and baking beans and bake in a preheated oven, 200°C (400°F), Gas Mark 6, for 15 minutes. Remove the paper and beans and bake for a further 12–15 minutes until the pastry is crisp and golden. Leave to cool completely. **THREE** Spread the pastry cream in the pastry case. Hull the strawberries, cut them into slices and arrange them in rows over the cream. Put the jam and water in a saucepan and heat gently until melted. Strain the jam through a fine sieve and brush it over the strawberries to glaze them. Serve in slices.

preparation time 20 minutes, plus chilling
cooking time 27–30 minutes

serves 8

note If you are making the pastry by hand sift the flour and salt into a bowl and rub in the butter with your fingertips until the mixture resembles fine breadcrumbs. Add the remaining ingredients and work them together to form a soft dough. Continue as above.

Pear and almond tart with chocolate sauce Pear, almonds and chocolate share an affinity and combine beautifully in this luxurious tart.

ingredients 1 quantity sweet shortcrust pastry dough (*see page 20*), 1 quantity chocolate sauce (*see page 112*), icing sugar, for dusting, vanilla ice cream, to serve filling 125 g (4 oz) unsalted butter, softened, 125 g (4 oz) caster sugar, 125 g (4 oz) ground almonds, 2 eggs, lightly beaten, 1 tablespoon lemon juice, 3 ripe pears, peeled, cored and thickly sliced, 25 g (1 oz) flaked almonds

method **ONE** Roll out the pastry on a lightly floured surface and use it to line a 25 cm (10 inch) flan tin. Prick the base with a fork and chill for a further 30 minutes. Line the pastry with baking paper and baking beans and bake in a preheated oven, 200°C (400°F), Gas Mark 6, for 15 minutes. Remove the baking paper and beans and bake for a further 10–12 minutes until the pastry is crisp and golden. Leave to cool completely. Reduce the temperature to 190°C (375°F), Gas Mark 5. **TWO** Make the filling. Beat the butter, sugar and ground almonds together until smooth and then beat in the eggs and lemon juice. Arrange the pear slices over the pastry case and carefully spread over the almond cream. Sprinkle with the flaked almonds and bake for 30 minutes until the topping is golden and firm to the touch. Remove from the oven and leave to cool. **THREE** Dust the tart with icing sugar and serve in wedges with the chocolate sauce and some vanilla ice cream.

preparation time 20 minutes, plus chilling
cooking time 55–57 minutes

serves 8

Mixed berry tartlets

These tartlets can also be made as one large tart. Use the pastry to line a 20 cm (8 inch) flan tin and bake for a further 10–15 minutes until set.

ingredients

1 quantity sweet shortcrust pastry dough (*see page* 20), 2 tablespoons apricot glaze, to glaze (*see page 102*), icing sugar, to dust **filling** 125 g (4 oz) unsalted butter, softened, 125 g (4 oz) caster sugar, 2 eggs, lightly beaten, 125 g (4 oz) ground hazelnuts, 175 g (6 oz) mixed summer berries (such as raspberries and blueberries)

method

ONE Divide the pastry into 6 pieces and roll each one out on a lightly floured surface. Use the pastry to line 3 x 12 cm (5 inch) fluted flan tins. Prick the bases with a fork and chill for 30 minutes. Line the pastry cases with baking paper and baking beans and bake in a preheated oven, 200°C (400°F), Gas Mark 6, for 10 minutes. Remove the paper and beans and bake for a further 8–10 minutes until the pastry is crisp and golden. Leave to cool. Reduce the temperature to 180°C (350°F), Gas Mark 4. **TWO** Make the filling. Beat the butter and sugar together until pale and light and then gradually beat in the eggs a little at a time until evenly combined. Fold in the hazelnuts. **THREE** Divide the berries among the pastry cases and spoon over the hazelnut mixture, spreading it flat. Bake for 25–30 minutes or until risen and firm to the touch. **FOUR** Reheat the apricot glaze until it is warm and brush it over the tarts as soon as they come out of the oven. Leave to cool in the tins and serve dusted with icing sugar.

preparation time 20 minutes, plus chilling
cooking time 43–50 minutes

serves 6

Mango and palm sugar tatin

Caramelized mangoes cook under a blanket of buttery puff pastry in this version of the classic French upside-down apple tart.

ingredients

350 g (12 oz) puff pastry dough (*see page 21*) mango topping 75 g (3 oz) unsalted butter, 75 g (3 oz) palm sugar, grated (or light soft brown sugar), ½ teaspoon ground mixed spice, 3 small mangoes, peeled, pitted and thickly sliced coconut ice cream 450 ml (¾ pint) full fat milk, 300 ml (½ pint) coconut cream, 2 star anise, 5 egg yolks, 75 g (3 oz) caster sugar

method

ONE Make the coconut ice cream. Heat the milk, coconut cream and star anise together until boiling. Remove from the heat and leave to infuse for 20 minutes, then strain. Beat the egg yolks and sugar together, then stir in the coconut mixture. Return to the pan. Heat gently, stirring, until the mixture thickens to coat the back of a wooden spoon. Leave to go cold and then freeze in an ice-cream maker according to the manufacturer's instructions (or freeze in a plastic container, beating at regular intervals until frozen). **TWO** Make the topping. Heat the butter, sugar and spice together in a 23 cm (9 inch) ovenproof frying pan until the butter has melted. Remove the pan from the heat. Carefully arrange the mango slices in the pan, fanning them from the centre outwards, to make 2 layers (these do not have to be exact). **THREE** Roll out the pastry on a lightly floured surface and trim to a round a little larger than the size of the pan. Press it down over the mangoes and into the edges of the pan and pierce a small hole in the centre. Bake in a preheated oven, 220°C (425°F), Gas Mark 7, for 20–25 minutes until the pastry is risen and golden. Leave to stand for 10 minutes before turning out on to a large plate. Serve with the ice cream.

preparation time 40 minutes, plus freezing
cooking time 20–25 minutes

serves 8

Kaffir lime tart

When baking the tart check after 5 minutes and then again at 1-minute intervals until it is just set. Overcooking can cause the filling to curdle slightly.

ingredients

1 quantity sweet shortcrust pastry dough (*see page 20*), icing sugar, to dust

kaffir lime filling 175 g (6 oz) caster sugar, 200 ml (7 fl oz) freshly squeezed lime juice (4–6 limes), 8 Kaffir lime leaves (or the grated rind of 3 limes), 3 eggs, plus 2 egg yolks, 175 g (6 oz) unsalted butter, softened

method

ONE Roll out the pastry and use it to line a 23 cm (9 inch) flan tin. Prick the base with a fork and chill for 30 minutes. **TWO** Line the pastry case with baking paper and beans and bake in a preheated oven, 200°C (400°F), Gas Mark 6, for 15 minutes. Remove the paper and beans and bake for a further 12–15 minutes until the pastry is crisp and golden. Set aside to cool. **THREE** Make the filling. Put the sugar, lime juice and Kaffir lime leaves (or lime rind) in a saucepan and heat gently to dissolve the sugar. Bring to the boil and simmer for 5 minutes. Leave to cool for 5 minutes and then strain into a clean pan. **FOUR** Stir in the eggs, egg yolks and half the butter and heat gently, stirring, for 1 minute or until the sauce coats the back of the spoon. Add the remaining butter and whisk constantly until the mixture thickens. **FIVE** Transfer the lime mixture to the pastry case and bake for 6–8 minutes until set. Leave to cool and serve warm dusted with icing sugar if wished.

preparation time 20 minutes, plus chilling

cooking time 33–38 minutes

serves 8

Danish pastries
Traditionally Danish pastries are made using a special yeasted sweet puff pastry. Here puff pastry is used as a quicker alternative.

ingredients 2 x 375 g (12 oz) blocks bought puff pastry or 1 quantity homemade (*see page 21*)

topping ½ quantity pastry cream (*see page 25*), 12 apricots, halved and pitted, 1 quantity egg glaze (*see page 133*), 25 g (1 oz) flaked almonds, 6 tablespoons light soft brown sugar, 2 large plums, peeled, pitted and diced, ½ quantity apricot glaze, warmed (*see page 102*)

method **ONE** Roll out the pastry thinly on a lightly floured surface and cut into 12 x 12 cm (5 inch) squares. Place on 2 large baking sheets. **TWO** Place a heaped tablespoon of pastry cream into the middle of 6 squares and spread over the pastry leaving a 1 cm (½ inch) border. Arrange 6 apricot halves over the pastry cream, brush the edges with egg glaze and scatter over some flaked almonds and soft brown sugar. Bake in a preheated oven, 200°C (400°F), Gas Mark 6, for 15–20 minutes until risen and golden. Place on a wire rack and brush all over with some apricot glaze. **THREE** Place a heaped tablespoon of pastry cream in the middle of the remaining 6 squares and top with the diced plums. Cut a diagonal slit from each corner of the dough into meet the filling, then take alternate points of the dough and turn them up and over to meet in the centre of the pastry cream, pressing together gently, to form a windmill shape. Brush the exposed edges of the pastry with egg glaze and scatter with almonds and sugar. Bake for 15–20 minutes until puffed up and golden. Brush with apricot glaze and leave to cool on a wire rack.

preparation time 1 hour
cooking time 75 minutes

makes 12 pastries

Apple, pine nut and muscatel strudel

Strudel, the German word for whirlpool, is a sweet filling wrapped in thin sheets of filo pastry. Fillings can vary using different fruits.

ingredients 12 sheets filo pastry, 65 g (2½ oz) unsalted butter, melted, custard or cream, to serve filling 100 g (3½ oz) muscatel raisins, 2 tablespoons brandy, 750 g (1½ lb) dessert apples, 75 g (3 oz) fresh white breadcrumbs, 50 g (2 oz) soft light brown sugar, grated rind of 1 lemon, 50 g (2 oz) pine nuts, toasted, 1 teaspoon ground cinnamon to dust 2 tablespoons icing sugar, 1 teaspoon ground cinnamon

method **ONE** Make the filling. Put the raisins in a bowl and cover with the brandy. Set aside to soak for 2 hours. **TWO** Quarter and core the apples and cut into small dice, put them in a bowl and add the breadcrumbs, sugar, lemon rind, pine nuts, cinnamon and the raisins and their juices. Stir well. **THREE** Lay 2 sheets of the pastry on the work surface next to each other and overlapping by about 2.5 cm (1 inch) to form a larger sheet of pastry. Brush with melted butter and then top with the remaining pastry, brushing each time with the butter. **FOUR** Spread the apple mixture over the pastry, leaving a 5 cm (2 inch) border. Fold the long sides over the filling. Brush with butter and roll up from a short side to form a Swiss roll. **FIVE** Transfer to a baking sheet, brush with the remaining melted butter and bake in a preheated oven, 200°C (400°F), Gas Mark 6, for 30–35 minutes until lightly golden. Combine the icing sugar and cinnamon and dust the strudel. Serve hot with custard or whipped cream.

preparation time 30 minutes, plus soaking
cooking time 30–35 minutes

serves 6

Glazed apricot tart

This simple fruit tart uses puff pastry as a base – make sure you press the pastry well down into the sides of the tin before trimming the edges.

ingredients

350 g (12 oz) puff pastry dough (*see page 21*), crème fraîche, to serve **filling** 75 g (3 oz) pistachio nuts, finely ground, 9–10 large apricots, halved, pitted and quartered, 2 tablespoons caster sugar **apricot glaze** 250 g (8 oz) apricot jam, 2 teaspoons lemon juice, 2 teaspoons water

method

ONE Make the apricot glaze. Put the jam in a small saucepan with the lemon juice and water and heat gently until the jam melts. Increase the heat and boil for 1 minute, remove from the heat and press through a fine sieve. Keep warm until it is needed. **TWO** Roll out the pastry on a lightly floured surface to 2 mm (⅛ inch) thick and use it to line a 25 cm (10 inch) flan tin, allowing the extra dough to overhang the tin. Press the pastry well into the edges and use a rolling pin to roll over the top of the tin to remove excess pastry. Prick the base with a fork and chill for 30 minutes. **THREE** Spread 2 tablespoons of the apricot glaze over the pastry case and scatter over 50 g (2 oz) of the ground pistachio nuts. Arrange the apricot quarters in concentric circles over the nuts, sprinkle with sugar and bake in a preheated oven, 220°C (425°F), Gas Mark 7, for 30 minutes. Remove from the oven and, while still hot, brush the apricots with a little of the glaze. Leave to cool. **FOUR** Sprinkle the edges of the tart with some ground pistachio nuts and serve warm with crème fraîche.

preparation time 20 minutes, plus chilling
cooking time 30 minutes

serves 8

Christmas mincemeat tart

Flaky pastry is similar to puff pastry, but has fewer layers. Puff pastry can be used instead if you don't want to make your own.

ingredients 1 quantity flaky pastry (*see page 22*), icing sugar, to dust **filling** 400 g (13 oz) jar mincemeat, 2 eating apples, peeled, cored and thinly sliced, 50 g (2 oz) dried cranberries, 1 quantity egg glaze (*see page 133*), 25 g (1 oz) flaked almonds **brandy butter** 125 g (4 oz) unsalted butter, 50 g (2 oz) caster sugar, 2 tablespoons brandy, 2 tablespoons double cream

method **ONE** Divide the pastry in half and roll out **ONE** piece on a lightly floured surface to a 20 x 30 cm (8 x 12 inch) rectangle. Put it on a baking sheet lined with baking paper. **TWO** Roll out the second piece of pastry so that it is slightly larger than the first. Dust it liberally with flour and fold it in half lengthways. Lay the folded pastry flat, with the folded side towards you, and use a sharp knife to cut slits at 1 cm (½ inch) intervals to within 1 cm (½ inch) from the top edge. Unfold the pastry and brush away as much flour as possible. Set it aside. **THREE** Spread the mincemeat over the smaller piece of pastry, leaving a 1.5 cm (¾ inch) border. Arrange the apple slices on top and scatter over the cranberries. Brush the edge of the pastry with water and put the other piece of pastry on top, pressing the edges together well. Knock up the edges by gently tapping with a sharp knife to form shallow grooves (this helps the dough rise) then flute the edges by making small indentations with the back of the knife at intervals of about 1.5 cm (¾ inch). Brush the pastry with egg glaze and scatter over the flaked almonds. **FOUR** Bake in a preheated oven, 200°C (400°F), Gas Mark 6, for 25–30 minutes until risen and golden. **FIVE** Meanwhile, make the brandy butter. Beat the butter, sugar and brandy together until pale and light and then stir in the cream. Chill until required. **SIX** Dust the tart with sifted icing sugar and serve warm, cut in slices, with brandy butter.

preparation time 45 minutes
cooking time 25–30 minutes

serves 8

Ricotta and candied fruit slice
This recipe was inspired by Valli Little, editor of the Australian food magazine *delicious* – she has kindly allowed me to adapt it for this book.

ingredients 350 g (12 oz) puff pastry dough (*see page 21*), icing sugar, to dust **filling** 250 g (8 oz) firm ricotta cheese, 75 g (3 oz) mixed candied fruit, finely chopped, 50 g (2 oz) dark chocolate, finely chopped, grated rind of 1 lemon, 1 egg, lightly beaten, 25 g (1 oz) flaked almonds

method **ONE** Roll out the pastry on a lightly floured surface to 2 mm (⅛ inch) thick and to a 22 x 30 cm (8 x 12 inch) rectangle. Put it on a baking sheet lined with baking paper. **TWO** Make the filling. Beat the ricotta until it is smooth and then stir in the candied fruit, chocolate and lemon rind. Spread the mixture down the centre of the pastry, leaving a 5 cm (2 inch) border down each side. **THREE** Lightly score the pastry along each side of the filling and fold over the pastry sides to cover the edges of the filling. Brush the pastry with beaten egg and sprinkle over the flaked almonds, pressing them down lightly. **FOUR** Bake in a preheated oven, 200°C (400°F), Gas Mark 6, for 25 minutes until risen and golden, remove from the oven and leave to cool. Dust the tart generously with icing sugar and serve in slices.

preparation time 20 minutes
cooking time 25 minutes

serves 8

Chocolate fudge tart This can be made in advance if returned to room temperature for 1 hour before serving. Use dark chocolate with at least 75 per cent cocoa butter.

ingredients
1 quantity sweet shortcrust pastry dough (*see page 20*), cocoa powder, to dust, vanilla ice cream, to serve **chocolate filling** 2 eggs and 2 egg yolks, 395 g (12¾ oz) can sweetened condensed milk, 300 ml (½ pint) single cream, 125 g (4 oz) dark chocolate, chopped, 2 teaspoons vanilla extract

method
ONE Roll out the pastry on a lightly floured surface and use it to line a 25 cm (10 inch) fluted flan tin. Prick the base with a fork and chill for 30 minutes. Line the pastry case with baking paper and baking beans and bake in a preheated oven, 200°C (400°F), Gas Mark 6, for 15 minutes. Remove the paper and beans and bake for a further 12–15 minutes until the pastry is crisp and golden. Leave to cool. Reduce the temperature to 150°C (300°F), Gas Mark 2. **TWO** Make the filling. Whisk the eggs and egg yolks together until smooth. Heat the condensed milk, cream, chocolate and vanilla extract together in a saucepan over a gentle heat, stirring until the chocolate has melted and the mixture is smooth. Whisk the chocolate into the eggs and pour the mixture into the tart case. Bake for 30–35 minutes until the filling is set. Cool to room temperature, dust with cocoa powder and serve in wedges with vanilla ice cream.

preparation time 20 minutes, plus chilling
cooking time 57–65 minutes

serves 8

Custard tart with blueberries
A simple custard tart adorned with fresh blueberries makes a lovely summer dessert. Strawberries and raspberries are good too.

ingredients 200 g (7 oz) plain flour, ½ teaspoon salt, 2 tablespoons caster sugar, grated rind of ½ orange, 125 g (4 oz) chilled unsalted butter, diced, 2 tablespoons water, 500 g (1 lb) blueberries, icing sugar, to dust **custard** 600 ml (1 pint) double cream, 1 vanilla pod, split, 3 eggs and 1 egg yolk, 75 g (3 oz) caster sugar

method **ONE** Make the pastry. Sift the flour and salt into the bowl of a food processor and stir in the sugar and orange rind. Add the butter and process until the mixture resembles fine breadcrumbs. Add the water and process until the ingredients just come together. Transfer to a lightly floured surface and shape into a disc. Wrap in clingfilm and chill for 20 minutes. **TWO** Roll out the dough on a lightly floured surface and use it to line a 23 cm (9 inch) fluted flan tin about 3 cm (1½ inches) deep. Prick the base with a fork and chill for a further 20 minutes. **THREE** Line the pastry case with baking paper and baking beans and bake in a preheated oven, 200°C (400°F), Gas Mark 6, for 15 minutes. Remove the paper and beans and bake for a further 12–15 minutes until the pastry is golden. Leave to cool. Reduce the temperature to 150°C (300°F), Gas Mark 2. **FOUR** Make the filling. Put the cream and vanilla pod in a pan and bring slowly to the boil. Remove from the heat and leave to infuse until cool, then scrape all the seeds from the pod into the cream (discard the pod). **FIVE** Beat together the eggs, egg yolk, sugar and cooled cream. Pour the custard into the pastry case and bake for 30–35 minutes until just set. Remove from the oven and cool to room temperature. **SIX** Dust the tart with icing sugar and serve cut in wedges with the blueberries.

preparation time 20 minutes, plus chilling and infusing
cooking time 57–65 minutes

serves 8

French apple flan

When cutting a round from puff pastry make a number of short cuts around the plate rather than drawing the knife around, as this can stretch the pastry.

ingredients

350 g (12 oz) puff pastry dough (*see page 21*), apricot glaze (*see page 102*), to decorate, crème fraîche, to serve **apple topping** 2 Granny Smith apples, peeled, cored and sliced, 1 tablespoon caster sugar, 25 g (1 oz) chilled unsalted butter

method

ONE Divide the pastry into 4 equal pieces and roll each out on a lightly floured surface until 2 mm (⅛ inch) thick. Using a 14 cm (5½ inch) plate as a guide, cut out 4 rounds and put each one on a baking sheet. Place a slightly smaller plate on each pastry and score around the edge to form a 1 cm (½ inch) border. Prick the centres with a fork and chill for 30 minutes. **TWO** Arrange the apples slices in a circle over the pastry and scatter over the sugar. Grate over the butter and bake in a preheated oven, 220°C (425°F), Gas Mark 7, for 25–30 minutes until the pastry and apples are golden. **THREE** Reheat the apricot glaze until it is warm and brush over each tart while still warm. Serve with ice cream.

preparation time 20 minutes, plus chilling
cooking time 25–30 minutes

serves 4

Deep-dish apple and blackberry pie
Apples and blackberries combine in this timeless classic. You can use frozen blackberries when fresh ones are not available.

ingredients 200 g (7 oz) plain flour, sifted, ½ teaspoon salt, 125 g (4 oz) chilled butter, diced, 2 tablespoons cold water, caster sugar, to dust filling 750 g (1½ lb) cooking apples (such as Bramley), 250 g (8 oz) blackberries, 2–4 tablespoons caster sugar, 25 g (1 oz) unsalted butter, diced, ½ teaspoon ground cinnamon, 1 tablespoon milk

method ONE Make the pastry. Put the flour and salt in a food processor, add the butter and pulse briefly until the mixture resembles fine breadcrumbs. Add the water and process again until the pastry just starts to come together. Transfer the dough to a lightly floured surface, knead gently and form into a flat disc. Wrap the dough in clingfilm and chill for 20 minutes. TWO Peel, core and thickly slice the apples and put them in a lightly oiled 1 litre (1¾ pint) pie dish. Add the blackberries, sugar, butter and cinnamon and stir well until evenly combined. THREE Roll out the pastry on a lightly floured surface so that it is a little larger than the pie dish. Brush the rim with water and put the pastry on top, pressing the edges together well to seal. Pierce a hole in the centre of the pie for steam to escape and brush the pastry with milk. Bake in a preheated oven, 200°C (400°F), Gas Mark 6, for 20 minutes. Reduce the temperature to 180°C (350°F), Gas Mark 4, and bake for a further 15–20 minutes until the pastry is crisp and golden. Dust lightly with sugar.

preparation time 20 minutes, plus chilling
cooking time 35–40 minutes

serves 4–6

note See the note on page 92 for making the pastry by hand.

Rosewater and cardamom choux buns

Rosewater is available from supermarkets and specialist food stores. Pour the syrup over the buns just before serving to prevent them becoming soggy.

ingredients

1 quantity choux pastry dough (*see page 23*), pomegranate seeds, to serve (optional) **cardamom syrup** 150 ml (¼ pint) fresh orange juice, 75 g (3 oz) clear honey, seeds from 3 cardamom pods **rosewater cream** 200 ml (7 fl oz) whipping cream, 1 tablespoon rosewater, 1 tablespoon icing sugar, 150 g (5 oz) Greek yogurt

method

ONE Line a baking sheet with baking paper. Spoon the choux pastry dough into a piping bag fitted with a 2.5 cm (1 inch) plain nozzle and pipe 12 rounds on to the baking sheet, leaving plenty of space between each one. Bake in a preheated oven, 200°C (400°F), Gas Mark 6, for 20 minutes until puffed up and golden. Remove them from the oven, cut a small slit in each one and return to the oven for a further 5 minutes to crisp up. Transfer to a wire rack to cool. **TWO** Meanwhile, make the cardamom syrup. Put all the ingredients in a saucepan and heat gently. Bring to the boil and simmer for 5–8 minutes until the mixture has reduced by about one-third and is syrupy. Leave to cool. **THREE** Make the rosewater cream. Whip the cream and rosewater together until stiff and then fold in the icing sugar and yogurt. **FOUR** Assemble the buns by cutting each one almost in half. Spoon or pipe in some of the rosewater filling. Arrange the buns on plates, drizzle over the cardamom syrup and serve with some pomegranate seeds if wished.

preparation time 25 minutes
cooking time 25 minutes

serves 4–6

Coffee profiteroles with chocolate sauce Serve the chocolate sauce while it is still slightly warm because it will set as it cools. Or warm through just before serving.

ingredients 1 quantity choux pastry dough (*see page 23*) chocolate sauce 100 g (3½ oz) dark chocolate, chopped, 50 g (2 oz) unsalted butter, diced, 1 tablespoon golden syrup coffee cream 300 ml (½ pint) double cream, 2 tablespoons made espresso coffee, cooled, 2 tablespoons Kahlua or Tia Maria

method ONE Line a baking sheet with baking paper. Spoon the choux pastry dough into a piping bag fitted with a 2.5 cm (1 inch) plain nozzle and pipe 12 mounds on to the baking sheet, leaving plenty of space between each one. Bake in a preheated oven, 200°C (400°F), Gas Mark 6, for 20 minutes until puffed up and golden. Remove from the oven, cut a small slit in each one and return to the oven for a further 5 minutes to crisp up. Transfer to a wire rack to cool. TWO Make the chocolate sauce. Put the chocolate, butter and syrup in a small bowl set over a pan of gently simmering water (do not allow the bottom of the bowl to touch the water) and stir until melted. Leave to cool slightly. THREE Make the coffee cream. Whip the cream, coffee and liqueur together until stiff. Cut the choux buns almost in half and spoon or pipe the coffee cream into each one. Serve drizzled with the chocolate sauce.

preparation time 20 minutes
cooking time 25 minutes

serves 4

White chocolate and raspberry puffs

You can use bought puff pastry or if you follow the recipe on page 21, wrap unused pastry in clingfilm and freeze for later use.

ingredients

350 g (12 oz) puff pastry dough (*see page 21*), 150 g (5 oz) raspberries, icing sugar, to dust **white chocolate cream** 200 ml (7 fl oz) single cream, ½ vanilla pod, 200 g (7 oz) white chocolate, chopped

method

ONE Roll out the pastry dough on a lightly floured surface until it is a rectangle 2 mm (⅛ inch) thick. Cut it into 6 rectangles, each 7 x 12 cm (3 x 5 inch), and put them on a baking sheet. Chill for 30 minutes. Bake in a preheated oven, 200°C (400°F), Gas Mark 6, for 15 minutes until the pastry is puffed and golden. Transfer to a wire rack to cool. **TWO** Make the white chocolate cream. Put the cream and vanilla pod in a saucepan and heat gently until it reaches boiling point. Remove from the heat and scrape the seeds from the vanilla pod into the cream (discard the pod). Immediately stir in the chocolate and continue stirring until it has melted. Cool, chill for 1 hour until firm and then whisk until stiff. **THREE** Split the pastries in half crossways and fill each with white chocolate cream and raspberries. Serve dusted with icing sugar.

preparation time 20 minutes, plus chilling
cooking time 15 minutes

serves 6

Caramelized onion and spinach tart

Use freshly grated Parmesan to add an intense flavour to the pastry in this savoury tart, which is great served warm or cold.

ingredients 175 g (6 oz) plain flour, pinch of salt, 75 g (3 oz) chilled butter, diced, 25 g (1 oz) Parmesan cheese, grated, 3 tablespoons cold water filling 25 g (1 oz) butter, 12 small baby onions, peeled and halved, 6 garlic cloves, peeled but left whole, 2 tablespoons balsamic vinegar, 250 g (8 oz) frozen leaf spinach, thawed, 200 g (7 oz) crème fraîche, 2 eggs, lightly beaten, 25 g (1 oz) Parmesan cheese, grated, salt and pepper

method ONE Make the pastry. Sift the flour and salt into a bowl and rub in the butter until the mixture resembles fine breadcrumbs. Stir in the Parmesan and then gradually work in the water to form a soft dough. Wrap in clingfilm and chill for 30 minutes. TWO Roll out the dough on a lightly floured surface and use it to line a 23 cm (9 inch) fluted flan tin. Prick the base and chill for a further 15 minutes. Line the case with baking paper and baking beans and bake in a preheated oven, 200°C (400°F), Gas Mark 6, for 15 minutes. Remove the paper and beans and bake for a further 12–15 minutes until it is crisp and lightly golden. Set aside to cool. THREE Meanwhile, prepare the filling. Melt the butter in a frying pan and fry the onions and garlic gently for 20 minutes until soft and golden. Stir in the vinegar and cook for a further 5 minutes. FOUR Squeeze out all the excess liquid from the spinach and chop it finely. Spread it over the pastry case and dot over the onions and garlic. FIVE Combine the crème fraîche, eggs, Parmesan and salt and pepper. Pour the mixture over the filling and bake, standing on a pre-warmed baking sheet on the middle shelf, for 20–25 minutes until golden and firm to the touch. Cool and serve warm or cold.

preparation time 30 minutes
cooking time 47–55 minutes

serves 8

Smoked haddock tart If possible use undyed smoked haddock rather than the lurid yellow-dyed fish that is available.

ingredients 1 quantity shortcrust pastry dough (*see page 18*), crisp green salad, to serve
filling 400 g (13 oz) smoked haddock fillet, 300 ml (½ pint) milk, 25 g (1 oz) butter, 1 onion, finely chopped, 1 garlic clove, crushed, 1 tablespoon mild curry paste, 1 tablespoon chopped fresh coriander, 100 ml (3½ fl oz) double cream, 2 eggs, lightly beaten, salt and pepper

method **ONE** Roll out the dough on a lightly floured surface and use it to line a 12 x 35 cm (5 x 14 inch) rectangular flan tin. Prick the base lightly with a fork and chill for 30 minutes. Line the pastry case with baking paper and baking beans and bake in a preheated oven, 200°C (400°F), Gas Mark 6, for 15 minutes. Remove the beans and paper and bake for a further 10 minutes until the pastry is crisp and lightly golden. Set aside to cool. **TWO** Meanwhile, prepare the filling. Put the haddock fillet, skin side up, in a frying pan. Add the milk, bring to the boil, simmer for 5 minutes and remove from the heat. Take the fish from the milk and set it aside to cool. Reserve 100 ml (3½ fl oz) of the milk. **THREE** Melt the butter in a clean frying pan and fry the onion and curry paste over a medium heat for 10 minutes until the onion has softened. Set aside to cool. Flake the haddock into the pastry case, discarding the skin and any bones. Scatter the onion mixture and coriander over the fish. **FOUR** Beat together the reserved milk, cream, eggs and some salt and pepper and pour the mixture over the fish. Bake for 20–25 minutes until the filling is puffed up and golden. Leave to cool and serve warm with a crisp green salad.

preparation time 30 minutes, plus chilling
cooking time 45–50 minutes

serves 4

Potato, mushroom and sage pie Slice the potatoes as thinly as possible for this pie or use the slicing attachment on your food processor, to ensure even cooking.

ingredients 2 quantities rich shortcrust pastry dough (*see page 19*) filling 5 g (¼ oz) dried porcini, 2 tablespoons boiling water, 4 tablespoons olive oil, 1 onion, finely chopped, 2 garlic cloves, crushed, 1 tablespoon chopped fresh sage, 500 g (1 lb) mixed mushrooms, 750 g (1½ lb) main-crop potatoes, thinly sliced, 50 ml (2 fl oz) single cream, 1 quantity egg glaze (*see page 133*), salt and pepper

method **ONE** Make the filling. Soak the porcini in the boiling water for 10 minutes until softened. Drain well, reserving the liquid, and finely chop the porcini. **TWO** Heat half the oil in a frying pan and gently fry the onions, garlic and sage for 10 minutes until soft but not golden. Add the remaining oil to the pan, add the mixed mushrooms and porcini and fry over a medium heat for 5 minutes until soft and golden. Season with salt and pepper and set aside to cool. **THREE** Divide the pastry into one-third and two-third pieces. Roll out the larger piece on a lightly floured surface and use it to line a 23 cm (9 inch) spring-form cake tin, allowing the pastry to overhang the sides. Roll out the remaining pastry to form a 25 cm (10 inch) round and use a small pastry cutter to stamp out a 2.5 cm (1 inch) circle from the centre. **FOUR** Arrange half the potatoes in overlapping slices in the base of the pie. Top with the mushroom mixture and cover with a final layer of potato. **FIVE** Brush the rim of the pastry with a little water and top with the pastry lid, pressing the edges together well to seal. Trim off excess pastry. **SIX** Combine the cream and reserved porcini liquid and pour it into the pie through the hole in the centre. Brush the lid with egg glaze. Bake the pie in a preheated oven, 200°C (400°F), Gas Mark 6, standing it on a pre-warmed baking sheet, for 1 hour until the pastry is golden. Cool for 2 hours and serve warm, cut into wedges.

preparation time 40 minutes
cooking time 1¼ hours

serves 8

Salmon, prawn and spinach pie
Make this creamy fish pie ahead of time for convenience and chill until required, returning to room temperature 1 hour before cooking.

ingredients
675 g (1 lb 6 oz) puff pastry dough (*see page 21*), 1 quantity egg glaze (*see page 133*) filling 25 g (1 oz) butter, 2 shallots, finely chopped, grated rind of 1 lemon, 2 tablespoons plain flour, 300 ml (½ pint) single cream, ½ teaspoon grated nutmeg, 250 g (8 oz) frozen leaf spinach, thawed, 500 g (1 lb) skinless salmon fillet, cut into cubes, 250 g (8 oz) peeled raw prawns, 1 tablespoon chopped fresh tarragon, salt and pepper

method
ONE Roll out half the pastry on a lightly floured surface to a 25 x 35 cm (10 x 14 inch) rectangle. Repeat with the remaining pastry. Cover with clean tea towels and leave to rest. **TWO** Make the filling. Melt the butter in a saucepan and gently fry the shallots and lemon rind for 3 minutes. Stir in the flour and cook for 30 seconds. Remove from the heat, stir in the cream and then heat gently, stirring, for 2 minutes until thickened. Remove from the heat and season with the nutmeg and salt and pepper. Cover the surface with clingfilm and set aside to cool. **THREE** Drain the spinach well and season with a little salt and pepper. Lay one piece of pastry on a large baking sheet lined with baking paper and spread the spinach over the top, leaving a 2.5 cm (1 inch) border at each end and a 5 cm (2 inch) border down each side. **FOUR** Stir the salmon, prawns and tarragon into the cooled cream mixture and spoon over the spinach. Brush the edges of the pastry with water and top with the other piece of pastry, pressing the edges together firmly. **FIVE** Trim the pastry to neaten and then knock up and flute the edges (*see page 103*). Brush with egg glaze and pierce the top to allow steam out. **SIX** Bake on a pre-warmed baking sheet in a preheated oven, 220°C (425°F), Gas Mark 7, for 20 minutes then reduce the temperature to 190°C (375°F), Gas Mark 5, and bake for a further 15 minutes until the pastry is risen and golden.

preparation time 30 minutes
cooking time 40–45 minutes

serves 6

Roasted vegetable tart
Use a large roasting tin to roast the vegetables in a single layer to allow even browning. Or cook in batches.

ingredients 1 quantity rich shortcrust pastry dough (*see page* 19) **filling** 1 large red onion, cut into wedges, 1 large red pepper, deseeded and thickly sliced, 1 large courgette, thickly sliced, 2 garlic cloves, chopped, 1 tablespoon chopped fresh rosemary, 1 tablespoon extra virgin olive oil, 300 ml (½ pint) double cream, 3 eggs, lightly beaten, 75 g (3 oz) freshly grated Parmesan cheese, 50 g (2 oz) pitted black olives, salt and pepper

method **ONE** Prepare the filling. Arrange the vegetables, garlic and rosemary in a large roasting tin to fit in a single layer, drizzle with oil and cook in a preheated oven, 230°C (450°F), Gas Mark 8, for 30 minutes, stirring from time to time, until roasted and golden. Leave to cool. Reduce the temperature to 200°C (400°F), Gas Mark 6. **TWO** Beat together the cream, eggs, Parmesan and some salt and pepper. Set the mixture aside. **THREE** Roll out the dough on a lightly floured surface and use it to line a 30 cm (12 inch) fluted flan tin. Prick the base and chill for 20 minutes. Line the pastry case with baking paper and baking beans and bake for 15 minutes. Remove the baking paper and beans and return to the oven for a further 12–15 minutes until the pastry is crisp and golden. Set aside to cool. **FOUR** Arrange the vegetables in the pastry case, pour over the Parmesan mixture and top with the olives. Bake for 35–40 minutes until golden. Serve warm.

preparation time 30 minutes, plus chilling
cooking time 1½–1¾ hours

serves 6

Mini-vegetable pies

Everyone loves a good meat pie, and many towns have their own pie shops. This version contains no meat but is delicious nonetheless.

ingredients 350 g (12 oz) shortcrust pastry dough (*see page 18*), 350 g (12 oz) puff pastry dough (*see page 21*), 1 egg, lightly beaten filling 4 tablespoons extra virgin olive oil, 500 g (1 lb) button mushrooms, quartered, 1 onion, finely chopped, 2 garlic cloves, crushed, 1 tablespoon chopped fresh thyme, 250 g (8 oz) carrots, chopped, 250 g (8 oz) parsnips, chopped, 150 ml (¼ pint) red wine, 500 ml (17 fl oz) tomato passata, salt and pepper

method **ONE** Prepare the filling. Heat half the oil in a flameproof casserole and fry the mushrooms with a little salt and pepper for 4–5 minutes until golden. Remove with a slotted spoon and set aside. Add the remaining oil to the pan and fry the onion, garlic and thyme for 5 minutes. Add the carrots and parsnips and fry for a further 5 minutes until softened and lightly golden. **TWO** Add the wine to the pan and boil rapidly for 3 minutes, then stir in the passata, mushrooms and more salt and pepper. Bring to the boil, cover and simmer for 20 minutes. Remove the lid and cook for a further 20 minutes or until the vegetables are tender and the sauce is really thick. Set aside to cool completely. **THREE** Cut the shortcrust pastry into 6 equal pieces and roll each out on a lightly floured surface. Use the pastry to line 6 x 12 cm (5 inch) individual pie dishes. Divide the puff pastry into 6 and roll each piece out thinly so that each piece is slightly larger than the dishes. **FOUR** Fill the pies with the cooled vegetable stew. Brush around the rim of the pastry with beaten egg and top with the puff pastry, pressing the edges together to seal. Trim off the excess pastry with a sharp knife and cut a small slit in the centre of each pie. Brush the tops with the beaten egg and bake in a preheated oven, 220°C (425°F), Gas Mark 7, for 25 minutes until golden. Serve hot.

preparation time 40 minutes
cooking time 1¼ hours

serves 6

Beef, oyster and ale pie

There is something very comforting about this traditional, slightly old-fashioned beef pie. You could make the recipe in small, individual pie dishes if preferred.

ingredients

1 quantity flaky pastry dough (*see page 22*) or 350 g (12 oz) bought puff pastry, 1 egg, lightly beaten **filling** 1 kg (2 lb) stewing steak, cubed, 1 tablespoon plain flour, 25 g (1 oz) butter, 1 onion, chopped, 1 garlic clove, crushed, 2 carrots, chopped, 2 celery sticks, chopped, 1 tablespoon chopped fresh thyme, 2 tablespoons extra virgin olive oil, 600 ml (1 pint) stout (such as Guinness), 400 g (13 oz) can chopped tomatoes, 2 bay leaves, 12 large raw oysters, shucked, salt and pepper

method

ONE Put the steak in a bowl and add the flour and plenty of salt and pepper, stir well to evenly coat the meat. **TWO** Melt the butter in a flameproof casserole and fry the onion, garlic, carrot, celery and thyme for 10 minutes until the vegetables are softened. Remove them with a slotted spoon. **THREE** Add the oil to the pan and fry the beef for 4–5 minutes until browned. Stir in the vegetables, add the stout and scrape any sticky bits off the base of the pan. Add the tomatoes and bay leaves, bring to the boil, cover and simmer for 1–1½ hours or until the beef is really tender. Discard the bay leaves and set aside to cool. Stir in the oysters and any juices. **FOUR** Oil a 2 litre (3½ pint) capacity pie dish. Roll out the pastry on a lightly floured surface to 2 mm (⅛ inch) thick and about 2.5 cm (1 inch) larger than the dish. Tip the stew into the dish and brush the rim with a little beaten egg. Lay the pastry over the top, pressing down well. Trim the excess with a sharp knife and knock up and flute the edges (*see page 103*). **FIVE** Cut out leaf shapes from the pastry trimmings. Brush the pastry lid with beaten egg and press the leaves into the centre of the pie to form a pattern. Pierce a small slit in the centre, brush with egg glaze and bake in a preheated oven, 200°C (400°F), Gas Mark 6, for 35–40 minutes until the pastry is risen and golden.

preparation time 1 hour
cooking time 2–2½ hours

serves 4

Crab filo tartlets
Filo pastry is now widely available commercially and can be found in either the chiller or freezer section of most large supermarkets.

ingredients
8 sheets filo pastry, 75 g (3 oz) butter, melted, green salad, to serve **filling** 500 g (1 lb) white crabmeat (fresh or frozen), 2 spring onions, trimmed and finely chopped, 2 tablespoons chopped fresh coriander, grated rind and juice of 1 lime, 3 eggs, lightly beaten, 300 ml (½ pint) double cream, ½ teaspoon five spice powder, salt and pepper

method
ONE Lay the pastry sheets flat on the work surface and cut them into 6 x 12 cm (5 inch) squares. Take 8 small squares, brush each with melted butter and press them into a 12 cm (5 inch) pie tin, arranging the squares at angles to line the whole tin and allowing the points of the square to point upwards. Repeat to make 6 pastry cases. **TWO** Pick through the crabmeat to make sure there are no pieces of cartilage. Put the crabmeat in a bowl, stir in the spring onions, coriander and the lime rind and juice. Beat together the eggs, cream, five spice powder and salt and pepper and stir into the crab mixture. **THREE** Divide the filling among the pastry cases and bake in a preheated oven, 200°C (400°F), Gas Mark 6, for 25–30 minutes until the filling is puffed up and the pastry is golden. Leave to cool in the tins and serve warm with a green salad.

preparation time 30 minutes
cooking time 25–30 minutes

serves 6

Breads

Fig and walnut bread
This lovely fruit and nut bread is enriched with the treacly flavour of molasses, and is a real teatime treat. Serve plain or toasted.

ingredients
450 g (14½ oz) white bread flour, sifted, 250 g (8 oz) wholemeal bread flour, 7 g (¼ oz) sachet fast-acting yeast, 2 teaspoons salt, 400 ml (14 fl oz) warm water, 1 tablespoon molasses, 125 g (4 oz) walnuts, toasted and chopped, 125 g (4 oz) dried figs, finely chopped

method
ONE Put the flours in the bowl of a food mixer and stir in the yeast and salt. Add the water and molasses, set the mixer to low and work the ingredients together to form a slightly sticky dough. Increase the speed to high and knead for 8–10 minutes until the dough is smooth and elastic. Add the walnuts and figs and knead for a further 2 minutes until evenly incorporated. Shape the dough into a ball and put it in an oiled bowl. Cover with a clean tea towel and leave to rise in a warm place for 1–1½ hours or until it has doubled in size. **TWO** Turn out the dough and knock out the air. Divide the dough in 2 and form each half into a small, slightly flattened round. **THREE** Put the rounds on a large, floured baking sheet, cover loosely with oiled clingfilm and leave to rise for a further 30–45 minutes until they have doubled in size. **FOUR** Use a sharp knife to cut a diamond pattern into each round and bake in a preheated oven, 220°C (425°F), Gas Mark 7, for 30–35 minutes until the bread has risen and sounds hollow when tapped underneath. Leave to cool on a wire rack.

preparation time 30 minutes, plus proving
cooking time 30–35 minutes

makes 2 round loaves

note If you are making the bread by hand bring the flours, yeast, salt, warm water and molasses together in a bowl to form a soft dough. Knead on a lightly floured surface for 8–10 minutes working the walnuts and figs in towards the end.

Cottage loaf This simple white bread is a great starting point for beginners.

ingredients 750 g (1½ lb) white bread flour, sifted, 7 g (¼ oz) sachet fast-acting yeast, 2 teaspoons salt, 1 teaspoon caster sugar, 15 g (½ oz) chilled butter, diced, 450 ml (¾ pint) warm water, extra flour, for kneading and shaping

method **ONE** Combine the flour, yeast, salt and sugar in the bowl of a food mixer. Rub in the butter. Add the water and with the mixer set to low work the ingredients until they just come together. Increase speed to high and knead dough for 8–10 minutes until smooth and elastic. **TWO** Shape dough into a ball and put in an oiled bowl, cover with a tea towel and leave to rise in a warm place for 1 hour until doubled. **THREE** On a lightly floured surface, knock back the dough, shape into an oval and press, seam side down in an oiled 1 kg (2 lb) loaf tin. Cover with oiled clingfilm and leave to rise for 30 minutes more until dough reaches the top of the tin. **FOUR** Bake in a preheated oven, 230°C (450°F), Gas Mark 8, for 15 minutes. Reduce oven to 200°C (400°F), Gas Mark 6, and bake for 15 minutes more until risen and hollow sounding when tapped underneath. Cool on a rack.

preparation time 30 minutes,
plus proving
cooking time 30 minutes

makes 1 large loaf

note If making dough by hand, bring ingredients together in a bowl to form a soft dough. Knead on a lightly floured surface for 8–10 minutes. Continue as above.

Multigrain loaf
This makes a dense loaf with a wonderfully nutty, seedy flavour. You can use whichever combination of mixed seeds you like.

ingredients 350 g (12 oz) wholemeal bread flour, 250 g (8 oz) granary flour, 125 g (4 oz) light rye or barley flour, 2 x 7 g (¼ oz) sachets fast-acting yeast, 2 teaspoons salt, 1 teaspoon caster sugar, 2 tablespoons each rolled barley oats, sesame seeds, poppy seeds, sunflower seeds and linseed, plus extra for baking, 500 ml (17 fl oz) warm water, 2 tablespoons malt extract egg glaze 1 egg, 2 tablespoons milk

method ONE Put the flours, yeast, salt, sugar, oats and seeds in the bowl of a food mixer. Add the water and malt extract, and with the mixer set to low work the ingredients until they just come together. TWO Increase the speed to high and knead the dough for 8–10 minutes until smooth and elastic. THREE Shape the dough into a ball and put in an oiled bowl, cover with a tea towel and leave to rise in a warm place for 1½–2 hours or until doubled. FOUR On a lightly floured surface, knock back the dough, divide in two and shape each half into an oval. Press into 2 lightly oiled 1 kg (2 lb) loaf tins, cover with oiled clingfilm and leave to rise for a further 30 minutes until the dough reaches the tops of the tins. FIVE Brush the dough with egg glaze, scatter over some extra oats and seeds and bake in a preheated oven, 230°C (450°F), Gas Mark 8, for 15 minutes, reduce oven to 200°C (400°F), Gas Mark 6 and bake for a further 15 minutes until risen and golden. Remove bread from the tins and tap gently underneath, if it sounds hollow the bread is cooked, if not return to the oven for a further 5 minutes and test again. Transfer cooked breads to a wire rack to go cold.

preparation time 30 minutes, plus proving
cooking time about 30 minutes

makes 2 x 1 kg(2lb) loaves

Wholemeal rolls You can make this recipe into a wholemeal loaf by shaping the dough into your preferred shape and baking it for 25–30 minutes until it sounds hollow when tapped.

ingredients 500 g (1 lb) wholemeal bread flour， 250 g (8 oz) white bread flour, sifted， 7 g (¼ oz) sachet fast-acting yeast， 2 teaspoons salt， 1 teaspoon caster sugar， 450 ml (¾ pint) warm water， 2 tablespoons milk

method **ONE** Put the flours, yeast, salt and sugar into the bowl of a food mixer. Add the water and, with the mixer set on low, work the ingredients until they come together to form a soft dough. Increase the speed to high and knead the dough for 8–10 minutes until it is smooth and elastic. **TWO** Shape the dough into a ball and put it in an oiled bowl. Cover the bowl with a clean tea towel and leave to rise for 1 hour or until it has doubled in size. **THREE** Turn out the dough on to a lightly floured surface and knock out the air. Divide the dough into 8 equal pieces and shape these into rolls. Arrange them well spaced apart on 2 large, lightly oiled baking sheets, cover with oiled clingfilm and leave to rise for 30 minutes until they have doubled in size. **FOUR** Brush the rolls with the milk and bake in a preheated oven, 220°C (425°F), Gas Mark 7, for 20 minutes until they are risen and sound hollow when tapped underneath. Leave the rolls to cool on a wire rack.

preparation time 30 minutes, plus proving
cooking time 20 minutes

makes 8 large rolls

note If you are making the rolls by hand bring the ingredients except the milk together in a large bowl to form a soft dough. Shape it into a ball and transfer to a lightly floured surface. Knead by hand for 8–10 minutes until the dough is smooth and elastic. Continue as above.

Rye and caraway bread

In northern Europe and Scandinavia bread is often made from a combination of rye flour and wheat flour, typically flavoured with caraway seeds.

ingredients

500 g (1 lb) white bread flour, plus extra for dusting, 250 g (8 oz) rye flour, 7 g (¼ oz) sachet fast-acting yeast, 2 teaspoons salt, 1 tablespoon caraway seeds, 450 ml (¾ pint) warm water, 1 tablespoon molasses

method

ONE Combine the flours, yeast, salt and caraway seeds in the bowl of a food mixer and make a well in the centre. Add the water and molasses and set the mixer to low. Work the ingredients together to form a soft dough. Increase the speed to high and knead the dough for 8–10 minutes until it is smooth and elastic. **TWO** Shape the dough into a ball and put it in an oiled bowl. Cover it with a clean tea towel and leave to rise in a warm place for 1½–2 hours until it has doubled in size. **THREE** Turn out the dough on to a lightly floured surface and knock out the air. Knead gently and shape the dough into a log. Put it on a large, floured baking sheet, seam side down, and cover with lightly oiled clingfilm. Leave to rise for a further 30–45 minutes until it has doubled in size. **FOUR** Use a sharp knife to cut 5 slashes into the top of the risen dough and dust the top with flour. Bake in a preheated oven, 220°C (425°F), Gas Mark 7, for 30 minutes until the bread is golden and sounds hollow when tapped underneath. Leave to cool on a wire rack.

preparation time 30 minutes, plus proving
cooking time 30 minutes

makes 1 large loaf

note

If you are making the bread by hand bring the ingredients together in a large bowl to form a soft dough. Shape it into a ball and transfer to a lightly floured surface. Knead by hand for 8–10 minutes until the dough is smooth and elastic. Continue as above.

Margherita

A hot oven, a preheated pizza stone or baking sheet and a well-floured wooden board for sliding the pizza dough into the oven, all help to produce an authentic, crisp-based pizza.

ingredients 1 quantity basic pizza dough (*see page 24*) topping 400 g (13 oz) can chopped tomatoes, 1 garlic clove, crushed, 2 tablespoons extra virgin olive oil, plus extra to drizzle, 2 tablespoons chopped fresh basil, ½ teaspoon caster sugar, ¼ teaspoon dried red chilli flakes, 150 g (5 oz) mozzarella cheese, sliced, 2 tablespoons capers, drained, 2 teaspoons dried oregano, salt and pepper

method **ONE** Make the pizza dough (*see page 24*). **TWO** Meanwhile, make the topping. Put the tomatoes, garlic, oil, basil, sugar, chilli flakes and some salt and pepper in a saucepan. Bring to the boil and simmer gently for 25–30 minutes until thickened. Adjust the seasoning and transfer to a bowl to cool. **THREE** Turn out the risen dough on to a lightly floured surface. Divide the dough in half and roll out one piece thinly to a 30 cm (12 inch) round. Put it on a well-floured wooden board. **FOUR** Top the dough with half the tomato sauce and with half the mozzarella, capers and oregano. Drizzle with a little oil. **FIVE** Carefully slide the pizza on to a preheated pizza stone or baking sheet and bake on the middle shelf of a preheated oven, at least 230°C (450°F), Gas Mark 8 or hotter if possible, for 10–12 minutes until the base is crisp and the topping is bubbling and golden. Repeat to make a second pizza. Serve hot.

preparation time 30 minutes
cooking time 35–42 minutes

serves 2

note If you like press the pizza dough into a shallow 30 cm (12 inch) tin and bake it on the preheated stone or tray.

Caramelized onion pizza
This is my version of a wonderful pizza I enjoyed on a recent trip to northern New South Wales – cooked in a wood-fired oven, the flavour was exceptional.

ingredients
1 quantity basic pizza dough (*see page* 24), 125 g (4 oz) baby rocket leaves, 1 tablespoon extra olive oil, squeeze of lemon juice, 15 g (½ oz) shaved Parmesan cheese **topping** 4 tablespoons extra virgin olive oil, plus extra to drizzle, 4 onions, thinly sliced, 6 garlic cloves, halved or quartered, 1 tablespoon chopped fresh sage, 50 g (2 oz) semi-dried tomatoes, 75 g (3 oz) pitted black olives, ¼ teaspoon dried chilli flakes, salt and pepper

method
ONE Make the pizza dough (*see page 24*). **TWO** Meanwhile, heat the oil in a frying pan and fry the onion, garlic, sage and some salt and pepper over a medium heat for 25 minutes until golden and caramelized. Set aside to cool. **THREE** Turn the risen dough out on to a lightly floured surface. Divide the dough in half and roll out one piece thinly to a 30 cm (12 inch) round. Put it on a well-floured wooden board. **FOUR** Top the dough with half the onion mixture and with half the tomatoes, olives and chilli flakes. Drizzle over a little extra oil. **FIVE** Carefully slide the pizza on to a preheated pizza stone or baking sheet and bake on the middle shelf of a preheated oven, on its highest setting, for 10–12 minutes until the dough is cooked. Repeat to make a second pizza. **SIX** Meanwhile, toss the rocket with the oil, lemon juice, salt and pepper and some shaved Parmesan. Serve the pizzas topped with the rocket salad.

preparation time 30 minutes
cooking time 45–54 minutes

serves 2

Grilled vegetable and pesto pizza

Here the pizza dough is pressed into a baking sheet giving it a foccacia-style feel. It is delicious served hot or cold.

ingredients

1 quantity basic pizza dough (*see page 24*), 1 red onion, cut into wedges, 2 courgettes, thinly sliced, 1 small aubergine, thinly sliced, 1 red pepper, quartered, deseeded and sliced, 4 tablespoons extra virgin olive oil, 150 g (5 oz) buffalo mozzarella cheese, diced, salt and pepper

pesto 50 g (2 oz) basil leaves, 1 garlic clove, crushed, 2 tablespoons pine nuts, ¼ teaspoon sea salt, 6–8 tablespoons extra virgin olive oil, 2 tablespoons freshly grated Parmesan cheese, pepper

method

ONE Make the pizza dough (*see page 24*). **TWO** Meanwhile, put the vegetables in a large bowl and add the oil and some salt and pepper. Heat a ridged grill pan and griddle the vegetables for 6–8 minutes, depending on their size, until evenly charred. Set aside to cool. **THREE** Make the pesto. Grind the basil leaves, garlic, pine nuts and sea salt with a pestle and mortar or in a food processor to form a fairly smooth paste. Slowly add the oil until you reach the required consistency (it should be soft but not runny). Add the cheese and pepper to taste. **FOUR** Turn out the dough on to a lightly floured surface and roll it out to a thin rectangle. Press it into a lightly oiled 23 x 33 cm (9 x 13 inch) Swiss roll tin. Spread 4 tablespoons of the pesto over the dough and scatter over the vegetables and mozzarella. Bake in a preheated oven, 230°C (450°F), Gas Mark 8, for 15 minutes until the base is crisp and the mozzarella has melted.

preparation time 40 minutes
cooking time 21–23 minutes

serves 2–4

note Store any remaining pesto, covered, in the refrigerator for up to 3 days.

Sourdough A soured 'starter' dough, made 3 days ahead, is added to the main dough, giving the finished bread its distinctive flavour. You will need a food mixer to make this bread.

ingredients sourdough starter ¼ teaspoon fast-acting yeast, 300 ml (½ pint) warm water, 350 g (12 oz) white bread flour, ¼ teaspoon caster sugar bread dough 750 g (1½ lb) unbleached white bread flour, 250 g (8 oz) fine semolina, plus extra for dusting, 7 g (¼ oz) sachet fast-acting yeast, 1½ tablespoons salt, 2 teaspoons caster sugar, 700 ml (1¼ pints) warm water, 2 tablespoons extra virgin olive oil

method **ONE** Make the sourdough starter. Dissolve the yeast in the warmed water, then stir in the flour and sugar until smooth. Cover with clingfilm and store in a cool, dark place for 3 days. **TWO** Make the bread dough. Combine the flour, semolina, yeast, salt and sugar in the bowl of a food mixer. Add 125 g (4 oz) of the starter dough (chill the rest for later use) and the water and oil. Work the ingredients on low until they just come together, increase the speed to high and knead for 5 minutes. Transfer the dough to an oiled bowl, cover with a clean tea towel and leave to rise in a warm place for 1 hour until doubled. **THREE** Cut off 125 g (4 oz) of the dough to add to the remaining starter. Tip the dough out on to a well-floured surface, divide in half and shape into two flat rectangles about 25 cm (10 inches) long. Place on to 2 floured baking sheets, sprinkle lightly with semolina, cover with lightly oiled clingfilm and leave to rise for a further 30 minutes until doubled. **FOUR** Bake in a preheated oven, 230°C (450°F), Gas Mark 8, for 15 minutes, reduce the oven temperature to 190°C (375°F), Gas Mark 5, and bake for a further 10–15 minutes until risen and golden and sounds hollow when tapped gently underneath. Cool on a wire rack.

preparation time 30 minutes, plus proving
cooking time 25–30 minutes

makes 2 oval loaves

Parmesan and basil rolls

Here the flavoured dough is shaped into rolls and pressed into a cake tin. They form a whole loaf as they bake so tear them apart to serve.

ingredients

350 g (12 oz) white bread flour, 125 g (4 oz) wholemeal bread flour, 1 teaspoon salt, ½ teaspoon caster sugar, 7 g (¼ oz) sachet fast-acting yeast, 50 g (2 oz) freshly grated Parmesan cheese, 2 tablespoons chopped fresh basil, 300 ml (½ pint) warm milk, 1 tablespoon olive oil

method

ONE Sift the white bread flour into the bowl of a food mixer and stir in the wholemeal bread flour, salt, sugar, yeast, Parmesan and basil. Make a well in the centre. Add the warm milk and oil, set the mixer to low and work the ingredients together to form a soft dough. Increase the speed to high and knead for 8–10 minutes until the dough is smooth and elastic. **TWO** Shape the dough into a ball and put it in a lightly oiled bowl. Cover with a clean tea towel and leave to rise in a warm place for 1 hour or until it has doubled in size. **THREE** Turn out the dough on to a lightly floured surface and knock out the air. Divide it into 8 equal pieces and shape each one into a small roll. Put them in a lightly oiled 23 cm (9 inch) spring-form cake tin, cover with oiled clingfilm and leave to rise for a further 30–45 minutes until the rolls just reach the top of the tin. **FOUR** Bake in a preheated oven, 190°C (375°F), Gas Mark 5, for 25–30 minutes until the bread is risen and golden. Turn out on to a wire rack and leave to cool. Tear the rolls apart and serve.

preparation time 30 minutes, plus proving
cooking time 25–30 minutes

makes 8 rolls

note If you are making the rolls by hand bring the ingredients together in a large bowl to form a soft dough. Shape the dough into a ball and transfer it to a lightly floured surface. Knead by hand for 8–10 minutes until the dough is smooth and elastic. Continue as above.

Rosemary and olive oil focaccia Light and airy foccacia is made by allowing the dough to rise three times rather than twice, as for regular bread dough.

ingredients 500 g (1 lb) white bread flour, 7 g (¼ oz) sachet fast-acting yeast, 1 tablespoon chopped fresh rosemary, plus extra for sprinkling, 1 tablespoon sea salt, plus extra for sprinkling, 275 ml (9 fl oz) warm water, 2 tablespoons extra virgin olive oil, plus extra for drizzling

method **ONE** Combine the flour, yeast, rosemary and salt into the bowl of a food mixer and add the water and oil. Set the mixer to low and work the ingredients together to form a soft dough. Increase the speed to high and knead the dough for 8–10 minutes until smooth and elastic. **TWO** Shape into a ball, place in an oiled bowl, cover with a clean tea towel and leave to rise for 1 hour or until doubled. **THREE** Knock back the dough on a lightly floured surface and roll out to form a round. Press the dough into a 25 cm (10 inch) ovenproof frying pan or cake tin. Cover with oiled clingfilm and leave to rise for 1 hour. **FOUR** Using your fingers press indentations over the dough. Cover with oiled clingfilm and leave to rise for a final 30 minutes until well risen. **FIVE** Sprinkle the dough with a little salt, drizzle with a little oil and scatter over some rosemary. Bake in a preheated oven, 200°C (400°F), Gas Mark 6, for about 25 minutes until risen and golden. Cool on a wire rack and serve warm.

preparation time 30 minutes, plus proving
cooking time about 25 minutes

makes 1 large loaf

note If making by hand bring the ingredients together in a bowl to form a soft dough. Shape it into a ball and transfer to a lightly floured surface. Knead by hand for 8–10 minutes until the dough is smooth and elastic. Continue as above.

Olive bread
Both olives and olive oil flavour this ring-shaped loaf. To make rolls, divide the dough into 8 and bake for 18–20 minutes until golden.

ingredients 550 g (1 lb 2 oz) white bread flour, 1½ teaspoons fast-acting yeast, 2½ teaspoons sea salt, 250 ml (8 fl oz) warm water, 50 ml (2 fl oz) extra virgin olive oil, 125 g (4 oz) pitted black olives, roughly chopped

method ONE Sift 500 g (1 lb) of the flour into the bowl of a food mixer and stir in the yeast and salt. Add the water and oil and, with the mixer set on low, work the ingredients together to form a soft dough. Increase the speed to high and knead for 8–10 minutes until the dough is smooth and elastic. TWO Turn out the dough on to a lightly floured surface, add the olives and the rest of the flour and knead into the dough. Shape the dough into a ball and leave to rise in an oiled bowl, covered with a clean tea towel for 1 hour until it has doubled in size. THREE Turn out the dough on to a lightly floured surface and knock out the trapped air. Shape the dough into a log and then roll it out to form a thin sausage about 60 cm (24 inches) long. Form the sausage into a ring, pressing the ends together, and transfer it to a large, lightly oiled baking sheet. Cover it loosely with oiled clingfilm and leave to rise for a further 30 minutes. FOUR Bake in a preheated oven, 220°C (425°F), Gas Mark 7, for 25 minutes until the bread is risen and sounds hollow when it is tapped underneath. Leave to cool on a wire rack.

preparation time 30 minutes, plus proving
cooking time 25 minutes

makes 1 large loaf

note To make the bread by hand bring the ingredients together in a large bowl to form a slightly sticky dough. Knead for 8–10 minutes on a lightly floured surface. Continue as above.

Pumpkin and sage bread

The vibrant colour and rich flavour make this the perfect bread for autumn when pumpkins are at their best. Delicious with vegetable soup.

ingredients

250 g (8 oz) peeled pumpkin, cubed, a few saffron strands, 100 ml (3½ fl oz) boiling water, 350 g (12 oz) white bread flour, 1 teaspoon salt, 1 teaspoon fast-acting yeast, 2 tablespoons chopped fresh sage

method

ONE Steam the pumpkin for 10 minutes until the flesh is tender. Drain it on kitchen paper to extract the excess liquid, then mash well and set aside to cool for 5 minutes. Soak the saffron strands in boiling water for 5 minutes. **TWO** Sift the flour and salt into the bowl of a food mixer and stir in the yeast and sage. Add the pumpkin and saffron liquid. Set the mixer to low and work the ingredients together to form a slightly sticky dough. Increase the speed to high and knead for 5–6 minutes until the dough is smooth and elastic. **THREE** Shape the dough into a ball and put in a lightly oiled bowl, cover with a clean tea towel and leave to rise in a warm place for 1 hour until it has doubled in size. **FOUR** Turn out the dough on to a lightly floured surface and knock out the air. Shape the dough into a small round and transfer it to a lightly oiled baking sheet. Cover it with oiled clingfilm and leave to rise for a further 30 minutes until it has doubled in size. **FIVE** Bake in a preheated oven, 200°C (400°F), Gas Mark 6, for 30–35 minutes until the bread is risen and golden and sounds hollow when tapped underneath. Leave to cool on a wire rack.

preparation time 30 minutes, plus proving
cooking time 30–35 minutes

makes 1 loaf

note If making the dough by hand bring the ingredients together in a bowl to form a soft dough. Knead on a lightly floured surface for 8–10 minutes until smooth. Continue as above.

Bacon and beer soda bread
Beer replaces the more traditional buttermilk in this version of Irish soda bread, giving it a wonderfully nutty flavour.

ingredients 125 g (4 oz) smoked bacon, finely chopped, 350 g (12 oz) wholemeal bread flour, 125 g (4 oz) medium oatmeal, 2 teaspoons baking powder, 1½ teaspoons bicarbonate of soda, 1 teaspoon salt, 300 ml (½ pint) light beer, 2 tablespoons vegetable oil

method **ONE** Dry-fry the bacon for 3–4 minutes until golden. Set aside to cool. Combine the dry ingredients in a bowl, add the beer, oil and cooled bacon and work the ingredients together to form a soft dough. Transfer to a lightly floured surface and knead the dough for 2–3 minutes until it is smooth. **TWO** Shape the dough into a flat round, about 18 cm (7 inches) across, and transfer it to a lightly floured baking sheet. Use a sharp knife to score into 8 wedges, cutting down about 1 cm (½ inch) into the dough. **THREE** Bake in a preheated oven, 220°C (425°F), Gas Mark 7, for 15 minutes. Reduce the temperature to 190°C (375°F), Gas Mark 5, and bake for a further 20–25 minutes until the bread sounds hollow when tapped lightly underneath. Transfer to a wire rack and leave until cold.

preparation time 30 minutes
cooking time 35–40 minutes

makes 1 small loaf

Yogurt, Cheddar and rosemary muffins

Savoury muffins are as delicious as their sweeter counterparts and are lovely served on their own or with soup or a stew.

ingredients 250 g (8 oz) wholemeal bread flour， 125 g (4 oz) white bread flour， 125 g (4 oz) buckwheat flour， 2 teaspoons salt， 1½ teaspoons baking powder， ½ teaspoon bicarbonate of soda， 2 tablespoons chopped fresh rosemary， 50 g (2 oz) melted butter， 2 eggs, beaten， 100 ml (3½ fl oz) natural yogurt， 100 ml (3½ fl oz) milk， 75 g (3 oz) Cheddar cheese, grated， 8 small sprigs fresh rosemary

method **ONE** Mix all the dry ingredients together in the bowl of a food mixer and make a well in the centre. Beat together the remaining ingredients (except the rosemary sprigs) and pour them into the dry ingredients. Set the mixer to low and work the ingredients until they form a sticky dough. **TWO** Lightly oil an 8-hole mini-loaf tin. Take large spoonfuls of the mixture and press into the prepared tins. Press a rosemary sprig into each one. **THREE** Bake in a preheated oven, 190°C (375°F), Gas Mark 5, for 20–25 minutes until risen and lightly golden. Leave to cool in the tins for 5 minutes, then transfer to a wire rack to cool.

preparation time 20 minutes
cooking time 20–25 minutes

makes 12 muffins

Chilli and Cheddar cornbread

American-style cornbread is traditionally baked in a skillet (or cast-iron pan), but it can just as easily be baked in a cake tin or even a loaf tin.

ingredients 75 g (3 oz) plain flour, 1 tablespoon baking powder, 200 g (7 oz) medium cornmeal or polenta, 1 teaspoon salt, 3 eggs, beaten, 300 ml (½ pint) buttermilk, 4 tablespoons sunflower oil, 125 g (4 oz) Cheddar cheese, grated, 2 tablespoons chopped fresh coriander, 1 red chilli, seeded and chopped

method ONE Sift the flour and baking powder into a bowl and stir in the cornmeal and salt. Mix together the eggs, buttermilk and oil and stir the mixture into the dry ingredients, using a wooden spoon to make a smooth batter. Finally, stir in the cheese, coriander and chilli. TWO Oil a 23 cm (9 inch) round cake tin and pour the mixture into the tin. THREE Bake in a preheated oven, 200°C (400°F), Gas Mark 6, for 35–40 minutes until the cornbread is risen and golden and a skewer inserted in the centre comes out clean. Leave to cool in the tin for 5 minutes and then turn out on to a wire rack to cool. Serve in wedges.

preparation time 20 minutes
cooking time 35–40 minutes

serves 8–10

Scones
It was with feather-light scones like these that my mother first ignited my love of cooking. High tea was a daily ritual in our house, it was also my favourite meal.

ingredients
250 g (8 oz) self-raising flour, 1 teaspoon baking powder, 50 g (2 oz) unsalted butter, diced, pinch of salt, 40 g (1½ oz) caster sugar, 75 g (3 oz) sultanas (optional), 100 ml (3½ fl oz) milk, 1 quantity egg glaze (*see page 133*), butter, jam and clotted cream, to serve

method
ONE Sift the flour and baking powder into a bowl and rub in the butter until the mixture resembles fine breadcrumbs. Stir in the salt, sugar and sultanas (if used) and make a well in the centre. Pour in the milk and gradually work the ingredients together to form a soft dough. **TWO** Turn out the dough on to a lightly floured surface, knead gently and shape into a disc. Roll out the dough until it is about 2.5 cm (1 inch) thick. Use a 7 cm (3 inch) pastry cutter to stamp out 12 rounds, re-rolling as necessary. **THREE** Transfer the scones to a lightly oiled baking sheet and brush the top of each with egg glaze. Bake in a preheated oven, 220°C (425°F), Gas Mark 7, for 10–12 minutes until risen and golden. Leave to cool on a wire rack. Split the scones in half and serve with butter, jam and clotted cream.

preparation time 15 minutes
cooking time 10–12 minutes

makes 12 scones

Hot cross buns

Toasted hot cross buns were a family tradition every Easter in our house, the smell as they cooked was so inviting. Why wait for Easter?

ingredients 750 g (1½ lb) white bread flour, sifted, 2 x 7 g (¼ oz) sachets fast-acting yeast, 2 teaspoons ground mixed spice, 1 teaspoon ground cinnamon, 100 g (3½ oz) raisins, 75 g (3 oz) cut mixed peel, 100 g (3½ oz) caster sugar, 350 ml (12 fl oz) warm milk, 50 g (2 oz) unsalted butter, melted, 1 egg, lightly beaten, 4 tablespoons apricot glaze (*see page 102*), piping paste 50 g (2 oz) plain flour, 1 tablespoon caster sugar, 3 tablespoons water

method **ONE** Combine the sifted flour, yeast, spices, raisins, peel and sugar in the bowl of a food mixer. Add the milk, melted butter and egg. Set the mixer to low and work the ingredients together to form a soft dough. Increase the speed to high and knead for 8–10 minutes until the dough is smooth and elastic. **TWO** Place the dough in an oiled bowl, cover with a clean tea towel and leave to rise in a warm place for 1 hour or until doubled in size. **THREE** Knock back the dough on a lightly floured surface. Divide into 12 equal-sized pieces and shape each one into a small bun. Press the buns into a lightly oiled 20 x 30 cm (8 x 12 inch) cake tin. Cover with oiled clingfilm and leave to rise for a further 30 minutes until the dough doubles. **FOUR** Make the piping paste. Mix the flour, sugar and water to form a paste and spoon into a paper icing bag. Pipe the paste over the buns to form crosses. Bake in a preheated oven, 200°C (400°F), Gas Mark 6, for 30–35 minutes until risen and golden, covering the tin loosely with foil if the buns start to brown. Remove from the oven, brush each bun with apricot glaze and transfer to a wire rack to cool.

preparation time 25 minutes
cooking time 30–35 minutes

makes 12 buns

Chocolate brioche buns

Traditional brioches are made in fluted moulds as individual loaves or as small buns. If you don't have small brioche moulds they can be made in a muffin tray.

ingredients

500 g (1 lb) white bread flour, 1 teaspoon salt, 7 g (¼ oz) sachet fast-acting yeast, 50 g (2 oz) caster sugar, 125 g (4 oz) unsalted butter, melted, 5 eggs, lightly beaten, 12 squares dark chocolate, 1 quantity egg glaze (*see page 133*)

method

ONE Sift the flour and salt into the bowl of a food mixer and stir in the yeast and sugar. Add the melted butter and eggs. Set the mixer to low and work the ingredients together to form a soft, sticky dough. Increase the speed to high and knead for 8–10 minutes until smooth and elastic. **TWO** Shape the dough into a ball and put in an oiled bowl, cover with a clean tea towel and leave to rise in a warm place for 1 hour or until it has doubled in size. **THREE** Turn out the dough on to a lightly floured surface. Cut off and reserve 250 g (8 oz) of the dough and divide the rest into 12 equal pieces. Shape each piece into a bun and then flatten it out, placing a piece of chocolate in the centre. Fold the edges over the chocolate, pinching them together to seal. Press the buns, seam side down, into 12 lightly oiled individual brioche tins. **FOUR** Take the reserved dough and divide it into 12 small pieces. Shape each into a ball. Make a small indentation in the top of each bun, brush with a little of the egg glaze and press a small ball of dough into each one. Cover the tins with oiled clingfilm and leave to rise for 30 minutes until the buns have doubled in size. **FIVE** Bake in a preheated oven, 190°C (375°F), Gas Mark 5, for 20 minutes until the buns are risen and sound hollow when tapped underneath. Remove them from the tins and leave to cool on a wire rack.

preparation time 30 minutes, plus proving
cooking time 20 minutes

makes 12 buns

Index

Acknowledgements

Executive editor Nicola Hill
Editor Emma Pattison
Executive art editor Geoff Fennell
Design 'Ome Design
Photographer Ian Wallace
Stylist Louise Pickford
Production manager Ian Paton